THE CHRISTIAN'S *ATTITUDE*
TOWARD WORLD RELIGIONS

THE CHRISTIAN'S *ATTITUDE* TOWARD WORLD RELIGIONS

AJITH FERNANDO

Tyndale House Publishers, Inc.
Wheaton, Illinois

The royalties payable on sales of this book have
been assigned to the Literature and Education Fund
of Youth for Christ/Sri Lanka, which exists to pro-
duce Christian literature in Asia and to provide educational opportunities for Christian workers.

All Scripture quotations are from *The Holy Bible,*
New International Version copyright © 1978 by New
York International Bible Society unless noted other-
wise.

First printing, April 1987

Library of Congress Catalog Card Number 86-51481
ISBN 0-8423-0292-1
Copyright 1987 by Ajith Fernando

To Nelun, God's gift to me, with joy and gratitude

CONTENTS

FOREWORD

The greatest challenge before the church is making Christ known to every creature. Nearly two thousand years have passed since Jesus commanded his followers to go and make disciples of all nations. Yet half the peoples of the earth still have not heard the gospel, and of those who have been exposed, many have only a superficial knowledge. With the expanding population and the present course of church growth, some estimate that there will be more unevangelized people in the world by the end of this century than there are persons living today. Clearly evangelism must take higher priority among those who believe that Jesus Christ is Lord of all, the only "name under heaven given to men by which we must be saved" (Acts 4:12).

Believing the gospel, however, is one thing; making it meaningful to unbelievers is another. Many sincere Christians who want to witness seem unable to relate to persons of different religions and cultures. If the Great Commission is to be fulfilled in their lives, they must learn how to effectively communicate their faith.

Ajith Fernando addresses this need with rare sensitivity and insight. Recognizing differences of worldviews, he lifts up the supremacy of the Word in Christ while, at the same time, feeling deep compassion for the lost multitudes unreached with the good news of salvation.

The author cuts to the heart of the matter with theological precision, yet he moves beyond creeds to the attitudes we have toward persons of unfamiliar ways. A feeling of superiority all too often is the real barrier to communication. In our pride, we fail to realize that, but for the mercies of God, we would be as those who have no hope. Keenly aware of this fact, Ajith approaches this task with humility and a deep sense of divine grace.

He has earned the right to be heard. As a practitioner of evangelism, he has lived and worked in a pluralistic society for many years. Enhancing his experience, he has studied the issues with a scholar's dedication, having earned graduate theological degrees from two revered institutions. Most of all, a love for Jesus Christ and the desire to make him known pulsates through his life. I know of few, if any, leaders on the contemporary scene who seem more in touch with the subject.

Reading these pages will help us sharpen our Christian witness to persons of a diverse religious heritage, but more important, it can enlarge our vision of the coming harvest when, at last, the gospel will be preached in all the world for a witness and our Lord returns in glory to reign over his kingdom. With this anticipation, it is a pleasure to commend this book to you.

Robert E. Coleman, Ph.D.
Director, School of World Mission and Evangelism
Trinity Evangelical Divinity School

PREFACE

The issue of how to relate to non-Christians is crucial to believers both in so-called Christian and non-Christian countries. Christians everywhere encounter non-Christians who may belong to a religion, such as Islam, or a cult, such as Mormonism. Or perhaps we may encounter secularists, who have no allegiance to any religion. Our contact with non-Christians tells us that there is much that is admirable in their lives. Many of them are convinced about their religions and are committed to them.

How should we regard the admirable qualities and religious beliefs of non-Christians? Can they find salvation through their own religions? What type of relationship should we have with the non-Christians we meet? Should we try to make them Christians? How must we witness to them? Certainly these questions are different from questions one might ask concerning people from Christian backgrounds. The focus of this book is on non-Christians.

This book is in two parts. The first is based on Luke's record of Paul's ministry in Athens (Acts 17:16-34). I chose this passage because it gives a most comprehensive description of Paul's attitude toward Gentile beliefs and his witness to Gentiles. The first part contains more than an exegesis of this passage. Though it is based on careful exegesis, from it we arrive at principles regarding attitudes toward non-Christians and our ministry among them. Much space is given to seeing how these principles apply to the situations we encounter in contemporary society.

The second part of the book deals with issues that do not directly emerge from an exegesis of the Acts passage, though most of these issues too are related in some way to the principles derived from this passage.

I know that many within the church will disagree with what I have written here. So a lot of attention is given to defending what I believe to be the biblical position on the attitude and witness to non-Christians in the light of the objections raised against it. Though I have read extensively from the writings of those who hold differing positions from mine, I have not quoted extensively from them, because I have sought to write a nontechnical book for a nonspecialist audience. The literature I have studied would not generally be accessible to or be on the level that appeals to such an audience. But this audience would nevertheless encounter the arguments presented in this literature through other contacts in society and the church. So I tackle the arguments, but don't quote directly from the writings. My quotations are generally confined to those whose ideas I've used and to whom I need to express my indebtedness.

A word about how this book came to be written might be helpful. The idea of writing a book on the topic of Christianity and other faiths came to me about eleven years ago. I knew then that I was not ready to launch out on such a project. But I started gathering material for it from that time. Over the past few years I have spoken in many seminars and conferences on evangelism and found that questions relating to the topic of this book were regularly asked of me. These inquiries helped to strengthen my resolve to work on this book.

Things came to a head about three years ago when I saw the film *Gandhi.* I was deeply moved by the heroism of the life of one of Asia's great leaders. This film was also a strong challenge to my belief in the uniqueness of Christianity. I saw here a non-Christian using principles found in the Scriptures in a more effective way than most Christians would. In fact, the "Christians" were the oppressors here, and my sympathies were with the oppressed, most of whom were non-Christians. On returning from the film, I sat at my desk until the early hours of the morning, working on my response to the film in the form of a talk entitled "Evangelism under Fire." This talk was gradually expanded over the next three years into this book.

I first taught most of this material to different groups of Youth for Christ leaders in Sri Lanka. This was an enriching experience because of the lively discussions that accompanied each session. The reader will sense that this book is written from a background of interaction with those of other faiths, which is a vital part of my own life and also of our ministry in Youth for Christ. I have also shared portions of this material with leaders of the Salvation Army, the Fellowship of Christian University Students, the Hospital Christian Fellowship in Sri Lanka, and the Youth for Christ staff in Southern Africa and Singapore.

It is my hope that this book will have a threefold effect on its readers. First, I hope that it will help them think biblically about non-Christians and their beliefs. Second, I hope it will increase their joy and their appreciation of the supremacy of Christ and his gospel. Third, I hope it will motivate them to witness to non-Christians, and do so effectively.

I am indebted to many people who helped me with this

book. I clearly sensed the influence of five teachers during my study and writing. My mother introduced me to Christ and first taught me of the supremacy of Christ. Having been a Buddhist for the first fourteen years of her life, to her the supremacy of Christ became a reality particularly precious.

Dr. J. T. Seamands, Professor of Missions at Asbury Theological Seminary, introduced me to the subject of this book. Having spent most of his life in India, where he steeped himself in the Asian culture, he was at one time a great Indian evangelist and hymn writer. Though he is an American, he has done more than anyone else to help me discover the glory of my Asian culture. His book *Tell It Well: Communicating the Gospel Across Cultures* is the classic nontechnical treatment on many issues relating to the mission of the church.

Another Asbury teacher, Dr. Robert E. Coleman (now at Trinity Evangelical Divinity School), was a model of commitment both to theology and evangelism. Dr. Daniel P. Fuller, Professor of Hermeneutics at Fuller Seminary, showed me the importance of the thoroughgoing application of Scripture which drives one to face difficult questions squarely. YFC leader Dr. Victor Manogarom of India is a living demonstration of the excitement of the call to evangelism. I discussed many of the issues in this book with him and profited greatly from his wisdom.

Miss Sandra Leitch typed most of the manuscript of this book as her voluntary contribution to the Kingdom of God. My wife, along with Mrs. Faith Berman, Mrs. Jayanthi Sivapragasam, Misses Edna Rodrigo and Radhika Sivapragasam, Mr. Victor Arachchi, and especially my secretary, Miss Helen Selliah, helped in numerous ways. Friends and relatives in Sri Lanka and abroad helped me take short breaks from my busy schedule to "hide" myself in their homes and write. Many friends and colleagues prayed this project through to its completion.

My biggest debt of gratitude is to my wife, Nelun. She believed in this book and paid the price of releasing me to write it during a period of much stress in our family due to the illness of our children. It is with great joy that I lovingly dedicate this book to her.

PART ONE

CHAPTER ONE
ATTITUDES OLD AND NEW

A missionary ready to return home on retirement after twenty-eight years of ministry in Sri Lanka was interviewed by Sri Lanka's leading English language Sunday paper. There he explained how he had changed as a person after coming to a multireligious country.

"I was rather intolerant of other religions at the time and thought that mine was the only true one," he said. "But all that changed during a visit to a Buddhist holy place, Anuradhapura." He said he experienced such a sense of peace that he felt he was truly in the presence of God. The difference in faiths did not matter. From that experience this missionary said he learned "the lesson that all religions, lived up to their highest ideals, have the common threads of love and compassion in them. So," he said, "from that moment my ministry became not creed but need."[1]

This missionary was reflecting an attitude that is rapidly gaining popularity in the church today. I have often heard both Christians and non-Christians say that what matters is not which religion one belongs to but whether or not he practices his religion devotedly. Let us look more closely at some of these new attitudes to other faiths.

SOME NEW ATTITUDES TO OTHER RELIGIONS

When considering the new attitudes to other faiths in the church, we see some who still hold to a form of the uniqueness of Christianity and some who reject this idea completely.

"Christianity is unique, but . . . ," some say. Some who believe that Christianity is unique would also say that salvation could be mediated through other religions as well. They claim that because Christ is the Savior of the world, his salvation is experienced even beyond the boundaries of the Christian religion. Non-Christians, they claim, receive salvation through the rites of their own religions, though it is Christ who saves them.[2] These "saved" people of other faiths are sometimes called "anonymous Christians" because even though they don't call themselves Christians, they are recipients of Christ's salvation.[3]

Perhaps the most famous presentation of this view is by a Catholic priest, Raymond Panikkar. In his book, *The Unknown Christ of Hinduism,* he speaks of the "hidden Christ of Hinduism. Hidden and unknown indeed! Yet present there."[4]

He wrote:

The good and bona fide Hindu is saved by Christ and not by Hinduism, but it is through the sacraments of Hinduism, through the message of morality and the good life, through the *Mysterion* that comes down from him through Hinduism, that Christ saved the Hindu normally.[5]

Another Catholic theologian, Hans Kung, has called non-Christian faiths the "ordinary" way to salvation whereas Christianity is a "very special and extraordinary" way to salvation.[6] Because of this belief in the special place that the Christian gospel has, people like Kung would encourage some sort of proclamation of the gospel to non-Christians.

"Christianity is an equal with other faiths," others say. The British Presbyterian theologian, John Hick, is a good example of another school of thought that rejects the idea that Christianity is in any way superior to other religions.[7] Hick says the different religions are "equals, though they each may have different emphases." He says Christian theologians have been making the mistake of placing Christianity in the center and then considering the other religions in relation to Christianity. He says God is the center. The religions of the world, including Christianity, reflect God in their own different ways. The differences in the religions are to be expected because they have grown out of different cultural situations. These differences must be affirmed as expressions of the different human types in the world.

Hick, then, does not advocate a single world religion, as the Baha'is do. The Baha'is set out to unify the religions of the world by combining the good points of the major religions. But they succeeded only in adding a new religion to the multiplicity of religions already found in the world. Hick, on the other hand, looks for the day when "the ecumenical spirit which," he says, "has so largely transformed Christianity will increasingly affect relations between the world faiths" too.[8] Then we would not try to convert those of other faiths to our faith. We would try to live harmoniously with each other, affirming our similarities and learning from each other.

The multireligious services to promote peace held in Sri Lanka are an evidence of this attitude. In these services, representatives of each religion pray for peace according to their rites. These services have been hailed as a great step forward in restoring harmony in the land. Evangelical Christians have stayed away from such services as they believe that there is only one mediator between God and men, Jesus Christ (1 Timothy 2:5), a statement the Apostle Paul made when explaining community prayer.

So evangelical Christians in this case have regarded non-Christian prayer as unacceptable in God's sight.

New Approaches to Evangelism. These new attitudes to other faiths described here could make it necessary to rethink the nature of evangelism, resulting in some new approaches to evangelism.

We often hear people, using some of these new approaches, say that the Christian's evangelistic task is to help the Buddhist to be a better Buddhist, or the Hindu to be a better Hindu. They say that the goal should no longer be to see the church grow numerically. Rather, it is to give birth to a harmonious community where people faithfully practice religion.

I once spoke in a seminar in Sri Lanka on the topic of the Christian mission of evangelism with a view to conversion. The speaker who followed me presented another view: "If a Buddhist comes to me and says he wants to become a Christian, I discourage him from doing so," he said. "I tell him, 'You have a great religion for which I have the highest respect. Go and study your religion and try to be a good Buddhist.' "

Others say that our enemy is not so much the non-Christian faiths but secularism, which has hit both the East and the West. They suggest that the great religions of the world should get together and combat this irreligiousness, because religion, be it Christian or Hindu or Muslim, is necessary for man to be complete.[9]

Others emphasize the biblical idea that our call is to help

people achieve the full humanity God purposed for them. They define Christian mission in terms of humanization. However, many advocating this approach place little emphasis on the need for individuals to be reconciled to God through faith in Christ. Salvation is viewed almost exclusively in terms of political liberation and socioeconomic development. So today there is a lot of talk about the "theologies of liberation."

TRADITIONAL EVANGELISM UNDER FIRE
It should now be evident that the new approaches to evangelism are very different from the traditional approach. According to the traditional approach, evangelism aims at bringing people to the point of leaving behind their past beliefs and practices so that they place their trust in Christ alone for salvation and join the church of Christ. This view has come under heavy fire in recent years for many reasons.

First, this view is regarded as being too narrow, ignoring the working of God in the other religions and the great values enshrined in them.

Second, the traditional view is said to betray an intolerant attitude of exclusiveness that is alien to the tolerant spirit of Christ.

Third, this view is associated with arrogance. They ask, "How dare you presume that Christians are the only ones on the right side?"

Fourth, the desire to convert people to "our side" is regarded as a vestige of the imperialistic attitude of the colonial rulers, where one group of people sought to subdue, conquer, and exploit another group of people.

This book will respond to each of these objections, but answering these objections will not be the book's primary aim. Rather, the aim will be to expound the biblical attitude to other faiths. What we have said about the new attitudes shows how important it is for us to study this topic afresh. First, we will study the attitude of that greatest of evangelists, the Apostle Paul, as reflected in his ministry in Athens, described in Acts 17:16-34.

PAUL'S ATTITUDE TO OTHER RELIGIONS (ACTS 17:16, 17)
The very first verse in this passage pictures vividly Paul's attitude to other faiths as of "a spirit provoked." Luke wrote, "He was greatly distressed to see that the city was full of idols" (17:16). The idols and the temples that housed them were beautiful works of art, reflecting the heights of Greek cultural achievement. But Paul was more impressed by the wrongness of idolatry than by the beauty of the idols. So he was "greatly distressed."

The Greek word *paroxuneo* translated "greatly distressed" is a very strong word from which we get the English word *paroxysm,* which is another word for fit or convulsion. It is often translated "provoked" (NASB, RSV). G. Campbell Morgan described the situation well: "In the midst of the beauty and the glory and the art and the philosophy and the history of Athens, proud and wonderful Athens, this man was in a rage, was provoked."[10]

Paul was reflecting here the same attitude to idols that his Scriptures, the Old Testament, reflected. It is the normal inward reaction of one whose heart beats to the pulse of God. Such a person's chief aim in life is the glory of God. Idols are an affront to God's glory, so he is provoked by them.

A very similar reaction is recorded in the diaries of Henry Martyn, who was a missionary to India and Persia (Iran). Shortly after his arrival in Calcutta he wrote in his diary,

"Let me burn out for thee." He once viewed a worship ceremony at a Hindu temple. He saw the worshipers prostrating themselves before the images and striking the ground with their foreheads. He did not view this with an attitude of academic interest as a typical foreigner would. Neither was he impressed by the devotion of these Hindus, as many Christians today are prone to be. Martyn wrote, "This excited more horror in me than I can well express."

His reaction to this horror is most significant. He said, "I thought that if I had words I would preach to the multitudes all day if I lost my life for it."[11]

Paul's reaction to his distress was similar. But unlike Henry Martyn, he "had words," for Paul knew Greek, the language of Athens. Luke recorded, "So he reasoned in the synagogue . . . as well as in the marketplace day by day with those who happened to be there" (17:17).

As the first verse in this section described "a spirit provoked," the rest of the passage describes "a spirit restrained." As we observe the ministry of Paul in Athens, we see that even though the idols provoked him, he did not show his provocation outwardly. Even when he mentions in his speech that he "walked around and observed [their] objects of worship" (17:23), he did not mention the provocation this observation aroused within him. Instead, he said that he concluded from the observation that "in every way [they] are very religious" (17:22). His speech was a controlled, carefully reasoned defense of Christianity (vv. 22-31).

In this Paul differed greatly from the prophets of the Old Testament. When the prophets observed idols, they too, like Paul, were provoked. But they reacted to this provocation by thundering angrily against idolatry. This was due to the difference between the audiences of Paul and the prophets. The prophets were speaking to wayward Jews who had received God's special revelation and so knew that idolatry was wrong. They needed to be upbraided for disobedience to God's revelation that they already knew.

The Athenians, on the other hand, had no such revelation. They needed to be convinced of the futility of idolatry and the advisability of handing their lives over to God, the Father of Jesus Christ. If Paul had thundered angrily against idolatry he would have lost his audience. The sophisticated Athenians would have viewed Paul as an eccentric fanatic and disregarded his message. So Paul used the method of reasoning carefully against idolatry and in support of the Christian view of God.

Both Paul's and the prophets' aim was at repentance from idolatry (see 17:30). Both were provoked by idols. The prophets saw fit to express this provocation with righteous anger. Paul saw fit to restrain his anger and express himself with reasoned arguments.

So here we see a twofold attitude of Paul to other religions. On the one hand there is a firm belief in the wrongness of life apart from Christ. On the other hand there is a respect for all individuals because they are intelligent human beings endowed by God with the privilege and responsibility of choosing to accept or reject the gospel. This caused Paul to reason with them about the truth of God. This combination of a strong conviction about truth and a respect for the individual surfaces many times in this book and forms one of the foundational principles in formulating our attitude to other faiths.

NOTES

1. Alfreda de Silva, "Change of Heart after Anuradhapura Visit," *The Sunday Observer*, March 18, 1984.

2. For a full discussion of this see Nihal Abeyasingha, *A Theological Evaluation*

of Non-Christian Rites (Bangalore: Theological Publications in India, 1979); and Patrick Kililombe, "The Salvific Value of African Religions," in *Mission Trends No. 5: Faith Meets Faith,* ed. Gerald H. Anderson and Thomas F. Stransky (New York: Paulist Press and Grand Rapids: Eerdmans, 1981), pp. 50-68.

3. Karl Rahner, "Christianity and the Non-Christian Religions," in *Christianity and Other Religions,* ed. John Hick and Brian Hebblethwaite (Glasgow: Collins, Fount Paperbacks, 1980), pp. 75-77.

4. Raymond Panikkar, *The Unknown Christ of Hinduism* (London: Darton, Longman, and Todd, 1964), p. 137.

5. Ibid, p. 54.

6. Joseph Neuner, ed., *Christian Revelation and World Religions* (London: Burns and Oates, 1967), pp. 52, 53.

7. John Hick, "Whatever Path Men Choose Is Mine," in *Christianity and Other Religions,* pp. 171-190.

8. Ibid., p. 188.

9. Leopold Ratnasekara, *Christianity and the World Religions: A Contribution to the Theology of Religions* (Ph.D. diss., Institute Catholique, Paris, 1982), pp. 140-144.

10. G. Campbell Morgan, *The Acts of the Apostles* (1924; reprint, Old Tappan N.J.: Fleming H. Revell Co., 1979), p. 411.

11. Constance E. Padwick, *Henry Martyn: Confessor of the Faith* (New York: George H. Doran Company, n.d.), p. 167.

CHAPTER TWO
THE PLACE OF DIALOGUE
IN EVANGELISM

In the last chapter we stated that even though Paul was provoked by the idolatry in Athens, his ministry there was characterized by a respect for the Athenians as being persons endowed by God with the responsibility of choosing to accept or reject the gospel. Luke used some key words to describe Paul's ministry in Athens, thoughts that buttress what we have been saying about Paul's dual commitment to proclaiming the truth and to respecting an individual's right to choose the path he would tread.

EVANGELISTIC DIALOGUES (ACTS 17:17, 18)
Verse 17 contains the first key word describing Paul's ministry: "So he [Paul] reasoned in the synagogue with the Jews and the God-fearing Greeks, as well as in the marketplace day by day with those who happened to be there." The word *reasoned* is a translation of the Greek word *dialegomai,* which carries the idea of discussion. From this word we get the English word *dialogue.* Luke used it often to describe Paul's ministry (Acts 17:2, 17; 18:4, 19; 19:9; 20:7, 9). He used it when describing Paul's preaching. So

it seems that when Paul preached there was a place for discussion.[1] His audience would have been given the opportunity to ask questions and respond in other ways to what he said.[2]

The second key word describing Paul's ministry also carries this idea of discussion: "A group of Epicurean and Stoic philosophers began to dispute with him" (v. 18). In some other versions the word *dispute* has been translated "converse" (NASB), "argue" (JB), and "debate" (TEV).

So it is clear that in his ministry Paul constantly got feedback from his hearers. Dialogue is particularly important in evangelism among non-Christians for many reasons.

First, our hearers may not be interested in listening to an evangelistic sermon. They are not Christians, and usually they have not invited us to speak to them. They may not even be interested in Christianity. Discussion draws them into active involvement in the gospel communication process.

Some months ago, YFC held an evangelistic camp for Buddhists who had come under the influence of our mission teams that had visited their villages. At this camp we had talks on poultry farming and health care. The Buddhist audience found these talks very interesting because the subject matter was so relevant to their daily lives.

I spoke twice about who God is and about man's relationship with God. My first talk became a somewhat unsuccessful battle to win the attention of my audience. It left me hoarse, exhausted, and disappointed over my failure to communicate.

For my second talk, I adopted the dialogic approach. I asked questions of my audience and let them give their views on the topics I was covering. I also tried to present the gospel very clearly. This time I had no doubt that I had their attention. I spoke for a longer time but was much less tired at the end of it. Earlier they were not interested in what I had to say. Now they were willing to give me a hearing because I had drawn them into the communication process by asking them also to speak.

Second, discussion helps in communicating to non-Christians because what they understand from a monologue-type evangelistic talk may be very different from what we intended to say. Their way of thinking is very different from the gospel way of thinking.

Some years ago I gave what I thought was a clear gospel message at a Youth for Christ club meeting. After the meeting was over I asked a Buddhist youth who was there what he thought about what I had said. He said he liked it very much and that his religion taught the very same things.

I thought I had given a message that clearly showed how different Christianity was from Buddhism! He had heard me clearly. But he put into my words meanings different from those I had intended. He processed my words through his Buddhist mind and gave them a Buddhist meaning quite different from the Christian meaning I had attached to them.

Through discussion we can find out what our hearer has understood and what he hasn't. We can find out what his misconceptions, objections, and questions are regarding the gospel. Having found these, we can adjust the way we present the unchanging gospel so that he has the best possible opportunity to respond to Christ.

Third, discussion helps arouse our hearers to consider what we are saying. Though our hearers may have their eyes fixed on us intently, their minds may often be quite passive—or active, thinking about a football match or something else far removed from what we are saying. Sometimes hearers find sermons very soothing or entertaining. But their lives are not changed through the preaching. There are those who are very happy when the preacher has given them a good scolding, but they leave quite unchanged by the message that should have provoked them to repentance. These are just a few examples of passive listening.

The preacher's desire is to touch not only the mind and the emotions of the hearer but also his will. It is the will that is involved in the lasting directional changes in one's life. The preacher's desire, then, is to bring his hearer to the point of asking, "Now what must I do?" Discussion often helps achieve this goal.

Discussion may encourage the hearer to apply the message he hears to his own life and help him move from being a passive listener to one who seriously considers the implications of what he has heard. For example, when we ask a person what his response is to what he has heard, he is forced to give it more than a casual hearing.

All this tells us that dialogue can be an important means of proclaiming the gospel. Of course, we know of discussion situations that get nowhere, where people argue on irrelevant points and avoid facing the basic facts of the gospel. But that is not because the discussion method is ineffective. It is either because the discussion has not been skillfully handled or because the one to whom we are speaking is not sincerely interested in considering what claims the gospel facts have on his life.

USING THE METHOD OF SOCRATES
Verses 17 and 18 remind us of Socrates, who was known to have used the discussion method of communication. An ancient description of Socrates reads, "He was to be seen in the marketplace when it was most crowded."[3] There he

would enter into conversation with those he would meet. This is what Paul did too: "He reasoned . . . in the marketplace day by day with those who happened to be there" (v. 17). Paul was in the city of Socrates, and so he used the method of Socrates. His message was different from that of Socrates, but his method was similar.

Paul had not always used the method he used in Athens. But when he came to Athens he adapted his method to fit in with the Athenian culture. We call this "contextualization." Contextualization takes place when the presentation and outworking of the gospel is done in such a way as to be appropriate to the context in which it is found. That context may be Athens or New York or a remote village in Sri Lanka. Contextualization becomes necessary whenever we work with a person of a culture different from ours. It is needed when an affluent person from a New York suburb tries to witness to one from a poorer inner-city neighborhood of New York, or when a highly educated urban Sri Lankan tries to witness to a rural Sri Lankan who has little formal education.

Contextualization must be distinguished from syncretism. Syncretism takes place when, in the presentation and outworking of Christianity, elements essential to the gospel are dropped or elements incompatible with the gospel are taken on in the efforts to identify with non-Christians. Syncretism took place when the pagan idea of white supremacy was adopted by the church so that it supported segregation. It takes place when a Christian, trying to maintain his friendship with a non-Christian, refuses to insist that following Christ is the only way to salvation. It takes place when a Christian participating in a peace march worships with the rest when they pass a Hindu shrine. It takes place each time a Christian turns to an astrological guide for direction in his or her life. It takes place when Christians condone abortion and euthanasia because of a secular humanistic approach to the sanctity of human life.

There is an essential core of the gospel that is above all cultures. And even if some features of this core clash with the culture in which a Christian lives and works, he cannot dilute them or compromise them. In our study of Paul's speech, we will see how a lot of what he said clashed with the thinking of the Athenians. He refused to be a syncretist. But he was a contextualizer. When he communicated the gospel in Athens, he used the communication style of the Athenians even though his content clashed with many of their beliefs.

We see Paul's style of contextualization even more clearly as we look at his speech in Athens (Acts 17:22-31). We note that here, as in Lystra (Acts 14:15-17), he did not make any direct quotations from the Old Testament, very different from his speeches before Jewish audiences. The Jews accepted the authority of the Scriptures, so he quoted them. The Athenians did not accept this authority, so he did not make any direct quotes. Yet his message was what it had always been—the centrality of Jesus as proved by the Resurrection, and the need to repent and make Christ Lord.

In fact, Paul's message in Athens was thoroughly scriptural. F. F. Bruce points out that it echoed "the thought and at times the very language of the Old Testament writings." Bruce says that "like the biblical revelation itself, his speech begins with God the Creator of all, continues with God the sustainer of all, and concludes with God the judge of all."[4] Paul always preached from the Bible. But if his audience did not accept the Bible, or know about it, he was seen to abstain from quoting directly from it.

We also note that, while Paul's language and ideas are

scriptural, the form of his Athenian address was most appropriate for his philosophically oriented audience. We will see later how he commented on their own religious practices, quoted from their own philosophers, and used their own logical style of argumentation in his attempt to persuade them to make Christ their Lord.

There are important lessons here for anyone trying to present Christ to non-Christians. We must find out the methods through which those in our audience usually get truth into their minds. In different cultures different methods become important. In the Tamil culture, with its rich heritage of rhetoric, oratory could be an effective means to proclaim the gospel. The Buddhists of Sri Lanka love drama and music and so their religious festivals give a high place to those two art forms. Christians could use drama and music effectively in preaching the gospel to them.

In our ministry we have recently had some key leaders who are working among Buddhists to get training in music and drama. But we had as teachers those who have distinguished themselves in the "secular" arts orbit. We could not find committed Christians who knew the secular art forms well enough. We were too bound to the Christian culture in our understanding of the arts. So we would fail to impact non-Christians effectively through our artistic presentations of the gospel. Our desire in all this is to present the gospel to the Buddhists in a form with which they are familiar.

We find that the highly westernized youth of Sri Lanka, whose religion is close to secular humanism, also like drama and music. But the type of drama and music that appeals to them is very different from what we use with the Buddhists.

Now the methods we use may formerly have been used by non-Christians in ways that dishonor God. But that does not disqualify the method. The method was not evil. It was the things for which the method was used that were evil. So William Booth, the founder of the Salvation Army, exclaimed, "Why should the Devil have all the good music?" and encouraged the setting of Christian words to popular music. Christians in Africa and Asia took the drum and used it effectively in Christian worship and expression, even though animists had been using it for demonic rituals for centuries before that time. There was nothing evil about the drum. It was the way it was used that was evil.

DIALOGUE IS A PART OF PROCLAMATION (ACTS 17:18)
The third key word describing Paul's ministry in Athens is *preaching*. "Paul was preaching the good news about Jesus and the resurrection" (v. 18b). This statement is actually a summary of the ministry of Paul described in verses 17 and 18, which we said was dialogic in style. The word translated "preaching," *euangelizo*, is one of three words commonly used in the New Testament to refer to evangelistic preaching.[5] It means "to bring," "to proclaim," or "to announce" good news. This verse tells us that even in his dialogue Paul was seeking to proclaim the gospel. John Stott says that "Paul's dialogue was clearly a part of his proclamation and subordinate to his proclamation." Stott also reminds us that "the subject of Paul's dialogue with the world was one that he always chose himself, namely Jesus Christ, and its object was always conversion to Jesus Christ."[6]

Many Christians today have a very different idea of interreligious dialogue. They see it as a conversation between people of different faiths that informs each other about their respective religious beliefs and practices. Different subjects are taken and discussed from each other's viewpoint. Up to this point a biblical Christian has no objections. There is nothing in Scripture to stop people from discussing each others' religious views. But our objection comes when we consider the goal of this dialogue. Many take it to be interreligious harmony, mutual understanding and enrichment—not conversion. Going into many contemporary dialogue situations with the desire to proclaim the gospel so that conversion will result is considered unethical. So an international leader on the new approach to dialogue says, "Any one who approaches another with an *a priori* assumption that his story is 'the only true story' kills the dialogue before it begins."[7]

But a biblical Christian always approaches a non-Christian with a desire to proclaim the gospel, having conversion to Christ as a primary aim. This is not simply because he wants the non-Christian to "join his side." It is because he knows that in Christ alone is man's hope for salvation, and love for the non-Christian causes him to desire his conversion.

Some would say that if we go into dialogue with the aim of conversion then it ceases to be true dialogue. But I must affirm that true dialogue can take place even when conversion is our goal. The Christian approaches the non-Christian in all humility. He listens to him with respect. He affirms what is admirable in the non-Christian's life. The non-Christian has an opportunity to share his views and beliefs, to present his objections to what the Christian says and to seek clarification. They speak as friends. The non-Christian senses that he is respected and that his admirable qualities are recognized. But despite that respect, he senses that the Christian desires to bring him to Christ out of a conviction that in Christ alone is there hope for his salvation.

Over the past few years I have talked to many Buddhists, Hindus, and secularists about Christ and about their beliefs. We have done so as friends with a respect for each other. In most of these conversations the non-Christians have done more talking than I have. But I have always sought to present Christ as the only hope for their salvation. They would soon have sensed that this was my aim. But few have objected to this procedure, even though many have disagreed with my insistence on the uniqueness of Christ.

NOTES

1. *Today's English Version of the Bible* (TEV) renders this word "held discussions."

2. Colin Brown, ed., *New International Dictionary of New Testament Theology,* vol. 3 (Grand Rapids: Zondervan, 1978), p. 821.

3. Cited in R. J. Knowling, "The Acts of the Apostles," vol. 2, *The Expositor's Greek New Testament,* ed. W. Robertson Nicoll (1952; reprint, Grand Rapids: Eerdmans, 1974), p. 365.

4. F. F. Bruce, *Paul: Apostle of the Heart Set Free* (Grand Rapids: Eerdmans, 1977), p. 239.

5. The other two words are *kerusso* (to herald) and *martureo* (to witness).

6. John R. W. Stott, *Christian Mission in the Modern World* (Downers Grove, Ill.: InterVarsity Press, 1975), p. 63.

7. Wesley Ariarajah, "Towards a Theology of Dialogue," *The Ecumenical Review of Theology,* XIX, 1 (Jan. 1977), p. 5.

CHAPTER THREE
NON-CHRISTIAN
RELIGIOUSNESS

Paul's evangelistic dialogue in Athens attracted sufficient attention to gain him an invitation to a meeting of a distinguished body known as the Areopagus (Acts 17:19a). This body was the "council which had oversight of the educational, moral, and religious welfare of the community."[1] The delegates asked him, "May we know what this new teaching is that you are presenting? You are bringing some strange ideas to our ears, and we want to know what they mean" (Acts 17:19b, 20).

Paul's response to the Athenians is the great speech which we will study in detail in this book. The record we have of it in Acts "is, of course, a brief report on an address which must have been much longer."[2]

POINTS OF CONTACT (17:22)
Paul began with an observation about the religiousness of the Athenians. "Men of Athens! I see that in every way you are very religious." Some have taken this statement to be a criticism and used the word *superstitious* instead of *religious* (see KJV). But this interpretation does not fit in with

the rest of the speech. So most modern translations prefer the word *religious*. While it is not a criticism, neither is it a compliment. Some have thought Paul was resorting to flattery to win his audience. But a second-century philosopher, Lucian of Samosata, who lived in Athens, noted in one of his writings that it was forbidden to use complimentary introductory statements when addressing the Areopagus, in the hope of securing its goodwill.[3] If Paul had resorted to flattery, he would have disqualified himself from further participation.

Paul was simply making an observation about the life of the Athenians. They were a religious people. The word *religious* essentially means "respect for or fear of the supernatural."[4] The form this religiousness took was idolatry, which provoked Paul to anger (17:16). Paul knew that idolatry would not save the Athenians so he argued against it in verses 24 to 29 and called the Athenians to repent of it in verse 30. But he also knew that behind this idolatry was a sense of respect for the supernatural that was implanted by God.

This sense of the supernatural provided Paul with a stepping-stone from which he could move into an exposition of the truth about Jehovah God. Paul had found a "point of contact" with the Athenians. They were in agreement with Paul about the reality of the supernatural world. Paul mentioned their religiousness in order to get the Athenians onto the same wavelength as he so that he could lead them along into the new truths he wanted to present to them.

In the same way, the Christian witness also must observe those to whom he seeks to communicate the gospel and look, as it were, for an airstrip where he can land in their territory, an opening in their lives through which he can win their attention.

THE UNKNOWN GOD

Paul went beyond finding a point of contact with the Athenians (v. 23). Through his comment about religiousness he won their attention. But he went deeper to identify their yearnings. He told them how he arrived at the idea that the Athenians were "very religious." He says he "walked around and observed [their] objects of worship." Then Paul singled out one of these objects of worship because it helped him in his task of introducing Jehovah God. He says, "I even found an altar with this inscription: TO AN UNKNOWN GOD." He saw in this the evidence of a deep unsatisfied yearning in the Athenians.

The Greeks attributed the various natural phenomena they encountered to the gods. Different gods were said to be responsible for their tribulations and their good fortunes, so they wanted to be on the good side of all the gods. But they were not certain that they knew all the gods, so they dedicated an altar to the unknown god "to ensure that no god was overlooked to the possible harm of the city."[5]

This altar was an admission by the Athenians that their knowledge of the supernatural was incomplete. Paul used this admission as a launching pad for his description of Jehovah God, who did complete everything. They set up their altar in an attempt to complete everything, but they did not know which god was able to do this. So he was described as unknown. Paul knew the God who completed everything without the assistance of any other gods. He introduced this God to the Athenians: "Now what you worship as something unknown I am going to proclaim to you" (v. 23).

DID GOD ACCEPT THEIR WORSHIP?

Paul said that the Athenians worshiped God as something unknown (17:23). Does this mean that this worship was acceptable to God? Some say that such a conclusion is implied by this statement, that worship of this nature can bring salvation to a person. The worshipers may not know who God is, but they are saved because they worship God.[6] Some advocates of this view would say that we still need to present the gospel because this is not the ideal way to worship God.

Yet this text does not leave room for us to imply that the Athenians' worship was accepted by God. N. B. Stone-house has pointed out that the emphasis here is on the ig-norance rather than the worship.[7] Paul was focusing on the confessed ignorance of the Athenians because that gave him a foothold for his proclamation of the gospel. He was not making any value judgments about the worship connected with this ignorance. Later in his speech he stat-ed that the ignorance was no longer excusable and that therefore God "commands all men everywhere to repent" (v. 30). Such a statement shows that this worship by the Athenians was not acceptable to God. We will show later that this is God's attitude to all worship apart from his rev-elation in Jesus Christ.

CHRIST FULFILLS THEIR ASPIRATIONS
Paul's handling of the worship of the unknown god tells us something very important about how he regarded other faiths in relation to Christianity. He saw these faiths as the expression of a thirst for God, but he knew that only Christ can satisfy that thirst. So he approached non-Christians with the belief that they were thirsting for God. Blaise Pas-cal described this thirst in terms of a God-shaped vacuum in man. The thirst expresses itself in various forms in differ-ent people, though some seem not to be aware that this thirst exists. In Athens it expressed itself in the form of an altar to an unknown god.

So we too approach non-Christians with the belief that the gospel fulfills their aspirations. Now these aspirations may take forms of which we do not approve. But we must look beyond the form to the emptiness without God that causes it and seek to show how Christ fills this void.

Fear of unknown forces is a very powerful controlling factor in the lives of many Buddhists and Hindus in Sri Lanka. They go regularly to astrologers, shrines, medicine men, exorcists, or such people, who claim to have power to control or direct supernatural forces. When the people are faced with sickness or some such trouble, they ask, "Is this because of a charm or an evil spirit?" If so, they want to counteract the evil forces, using whatever means available to them.

Some rationalists, and even some evangelicals, scoff at these practices and say that they are caused by one's imagination. But this attitude is both unwise and incorrect. It is unwise because we cannot so easily dismiss such deeply ingrained feelings in people. If we dismiss them that easily, they would also very easily dismiss us as having nothing relevant to say to them. It is incorrect because the Bible clearly tells us that there are various supernatural powers at work in the world. Even Christians battle with these forces (Ephesians 6:12).

The biblical approach to fear of the supernatural and its manifestations is to show that our God is more powerful. The Bible teaches that because God is maker of heaven and earth, all forces are subject to him. So the method of the Christian witness is to recognize the questions and aspirations these people have and show that Christ is the answer to these aspirations.

Some people may object to this method of witness by saying that we must emphasize man's basic question, which is his need for a relationship with God, a relationship he does not experience because of sin. We agree. But many don't recognize that this is their basic question. We may tell a non-Christian the moment we meet him that he needs to have a relationship with God, and for that he must repent of his sin. His response may be that he does not believe he has such a need. There are other needs, however, which he has and recognizes, such as the need to be free from the influence of evil forces. Now we can start with this question and from it direct him to the most basic question, that of his relationship with God, which is hindered due to sin. We must at some stage arrive at this basic question. But we may not start with it, because if we do, he may dismiss us as having nothing to say that is of relevance to his life.

The Christian is always looking for the aspirations of non-Christians and exploring how he could show that Christ fulfills those aspirations. We believe Christ is the answer. But we must also ask what is the question. The question in a person's mind may not be what we think it is or what we think it should be.

Does this apply also to self-sufficient, secularized Western people? Do they ask such questions? They don't feel they need religion. They feel quite adequate to face the challenges of life without God's help. So we may conclude that they are not asking any questions of religious significance. The problem may be that we are looking in the wrong place. Our life-style is so different from theirs that we don't know the deep yearnings of their hearts. They do have religious aspirations. But those aspirations take forms that we may not recognize as being religious.

All this shows us how important it is for us to understand the non-Christian world. We do this in different ways. One way is by befriending non-Christians and by being available to help when they are in need. By genuine concern for them and close contact with them, we are able to get a feel for their joys and sorrows, their aspirations and questions. Another way to understand the non-Christian world is through the media. Literature, music, drama, film, television, and the news media give us important information about the non-Christian world and its thinking. They are important to us in spite of all that is unchristian about them.

FROM QUESTIONS TO ANSWERS (17:24-31)

It is heartening today to see many Christians trying to identify with people's questions and yearnings. But it is only a first step in the process of proclaiming the gospel. Some of the music, drama, film, and preaching coming out of the church today has been eminently successful in analyzing the way people feel and live in today's society. But these presentations are often weak in expounding the solution to the problems they have so successfully portrayed.

It is not enough to use our creativity in analyzing the human predicament. We must expound the gospel in such a way that our hearers know that the gospel is the answer to their questions. Often our methods of expounding the gospel are so stereotyped and plain that we lose our hearers in the process. They warm up to our analysis of the problem, but our solution to the problem leaves them cold. They identify with the problem, but have no desire to identify with the solution.

Here again, Paul is a model for us. His exposition of the gospel (17:24-31) was as relevant to the Athenians as was his analysis of their aspirations. His exposition was thoroughly biblical. It was the same message he preached in other places. He presented Jesus and the Resurrection and ended with a call to repentance. But the way he presented this unchanging gospel was very appropriate to his audience in that it was philosophical in style. He constantly interacted with the beliefs and practices of the Athenians. He even quoted from the writings of their philosophers.

From Paul's example, then, we see some important keys to effective witness among non-Christians. We must know the gospel thoroughly and communicate it faithfully and clearly. We must also know the world thoroughly. This knowledge of the world becomes the context in which we present the gospel. So when we proclaim the gospel, we constantly interact with the aspirations, beliefs, and practices of our audience. A good witness, then, is a student of both the Word and the world.

NOTES

1. Everett F. Harrison, *Acts: The Expanding Church* (Chicago: Moody Press, 1975), p. 269.

2. E. M. Blaiklock, *The Acts of the Apostles, The Tyndale New Testament Commentaries* (Grand Rapids: Eerdmans, 1959), p. 140.

3. Cited in F. F. Bruce, *The Book of Acts, New International Commentary on the New Testament* (Grand Rapids: Eerdmans, 1954), p. 355.

4. Alan Richardson, "Superstition," in *A Theological Word Book of the Bible,* ed. Alan Richardson (London: SCM Press Ltd., 1950), p. 253.

5. Blaiklock, *Acts,* p. 140.

6. Raymond Pannikar, *The Unknown Christ of Hinduism* (London: Darton, Longman, and Todd, 1964), p. 253.

7. Cited in Bruce, *Acts,* p. 356.

CHAPTER FOUR
ESTABLISHING
THE FACT OF GOD

We have seen how Paul approached his audience in Athens, using their own aspirations as a point of contact. He then described the God whom he had identified as the fulfillment of their aspirations. Acts 17:24-29 is an exposition of Paul's beliefs about what God is like. Paul did a similar thing earlier when he preached in Lystra (Acts 14:15). Paul's message was founded upon the truths about who God is and what he has done. The people did not know much about God, so before he asked them to respond to God's saving activity, he needed to explain the basic facts about God, facts that Christians may take for granted.

When Paul preached to the Jews and God-fearers at the synagogue in Antioch of Pisidia, he did not need to explain such basic things as the fact that God is Creator. There too he began his message by appealing to the activity of God. But there he focused on God's activity in the history of Israel (Acts 13:16-22). All this shows how very important it is to establish a foundation of facts about God before we present God's way of salvation for man.

MISCONCEPTIONS ABOUT GOD

It is particularly important to establish the truth about God when relating to non-Christians because of the misconceptions they have about God. The Athenians were idolators; so in this passage we see that while Paul explained who God is, he also showed the futility of idolatry (Acts 17:24-29). He needed to do this because he wanted to show the Athenians that there is one true supreme God, who alone deserves man's total allegiance. After establishing this fact (17:24-29), he could present the gospel of redemption (17:30, 31).

Similarly, the non-Christians we seek to witness to have many misconceptions about God. The secular humanist thinks the idea of God is a crutch, perhaps needed by weak people. One who has achieved his full human potential is regarded as not needing such a crutch. If there is a God and if he is personal, then he is a grandfather-like figure not in touch with what is happening in the "real world." Or perhaps he is just that force that was responsible for setting in motion the process of evolution. If so, he is impersonal, and we do not need to worry about relating to him. When we witness to a secular humanist, we need to correct these misconceptions.

The scientific materialist claims that the advances of science have shown that there is no God. The world could have evolved to its present state without the aid of a divine intelligence. We need to demonstrate to him that the evidence for God's existence can withstand the assaults it faces from certain quarters of the scientific community. As Paul bluntly put it, "We demolish arguments and every pretension that sets itself up against the knowledge of God" (2 Corinthians 10:5).

Many Buddhists think of the gods as inferior beings, who have even paid homage to the Buddha. They may perhaps be needed for protection. But they do not see a need to go to the extent of handing over their lives to these gods. The Christian witness needs to show the Buddhist the difference between the gods he knows and the Supreme God.

The Muslims place so much emphasis on the transcendence of God that they can visualize man more as a slave of God than as a son. They need to be shown the love of God who, while maintaining his transcendence and holiness, stooped down (became immanent) to redeem men and make them his dearly beloved children. We, however, often fail to establish the fact of God in our presentation of the gospel to non-Christians. We begin with a statement such as "God loves you" and proceed to build on that. But our hearers don't have even an elementary knowledge of who God is. Is it any wonder that our presentation of the gospel is often ineffective?

CREATOR AND LORD (17:24a)
Paul began his description of God by presenting him as Creator and Lord: "The God who made the world and everything in it is the Lord of heaven and earth" (17:24a).

Creation and lordship are two important foundations of the Christian gospel and are very important in our witness to non-Christians. They were important to Paul when he preached to the Athenians, who had many gods. Paul needed to show them that the God he was presenting was the only God that mattered. He was above all their gods.

Such is the case with the Buddhist, too. To him the gods are not all-powerful. They may even be inferior to the Buddha. They need to be shown that because this God is Creator and Lord, he is above every other god, even above the Buddha. Why then worship or follow an inferior being when we can follow the Supreme Being?

The idea of the Supreme God being Creator was something very contrary to the thinking of most of Paul's audience in Athens. They saw the material world as impure. Therefore, they believed that "the Supreme Being was too pure to come into polluting contact with the material order."[1] They said that a master workman (or *demiurge*), who is inferior to the Supreme Being, fashioned the world.

Christianity presents the very different belief that God is Creator. Implied in this is the belief that because God created the world, it can be a good place. Here Christianity clashes not only with Greek religion but also with some of the religions of the world today. The Buddhist says that because the world is full of impure desires we must overcome all earthly desire until we become people without human desire—a state very different from the human state. Buddhism advocates the annihilation of human desire because such desire is evil.

Christianity, on the other hand, sees human desire as something good because it was created by God. Indeed, it is tarnished because of sin, but we don't have to destroy it in order to be saved. We rather surrender it to its Creator and let him redeem it. So, when God saves us, he does not destroy our humanity. He makes us fully human.

The doctrine of creation also challenges the beliefs of the hedonist. Hedonists see the chief good of man lying in the pursuit of pleasure. Whereas the ascetic says we must destroy desire, and the Christian says we must surrender desire to God so that he may redeem it, the hedonist says we must indulge desire. The playboy philosophy proclaims, "Don't give temptation a second thought; give in at the first!"

But the hedonist cannot be fulfilled through his relentless pursuit of pleasure. When God created life, he also determined the means through which one could be fulfilled in life. To deviate from his plan would be to invite unfulfillment.

The doctrines of creation and God's lordship have something significant to say to the secularist, too. He has built round himself an edifice of self-sufficiency, which eliminates the need for a Savior God. He scoffs at the idea of a loving God, wooing him to come and receive his salvation. Such is needed only for weaklings who are unable to cope with the challenges of life. This is the response I once received from a successful businessman, who prided himself on being a "self-made man," after I had preached on the love of God, using the parable of the prodigal son.

The self-sufficient secularist needs to be confronted with the all-powerful Lord of creation. He needs to know that all his efforts will not yield an authentic life because he has ignored the principles of the Lord of life. He needs to be reminded that God is the ultimate controller of history, the "boss" of the universe whom he will one day have to face at an awesome throne of judgment and answer for the way he lived. His edifice of self-sufficiency needs to crumble through his realizing his littleness in comparison to God. Then he will admit he needs God, which is the first step to saving faith.

GOD'S SELF-SUFFICIENCY (17:24, 25)
Paul's next three statements proclaim God's self-sufficiency. First, he "does not live in temples built by hands" (v. 24b). This statement, of course, is a "bold denial of the validity of the famous temples clustered round him."[2] Paul was not afraid to clash with the thinking people of his audience. If Paul was to bring the Athenians to accept the good news of the gospel, he first had to destroy those beliefs that cannot coexist with the gospel. Paul had earlier

found points of contact with the Athenians. He did so later. He was not afraid to agree with his audience when he could, for his sharing of the gospel was not a competitive argument he was having with them. His aim was to direct his audience to accept the truth. He affirmed whatever glimmerings of truth they already had. But he knew that when he presented truth, he also had to show that the things that clash with the truth were untrue. And all non-Christian systems are untrue at their heart.

Paul's next statement also denied the validity of the Athenian religious practices: "He is not served by human hands, as if he needed anything" (17:25a). God does not need man's favors. He is self-sufficient. Then Paul substantiated his statement about God's self-sufficiency: "Because he himself gives all men life and breath and everything else" (17:25b). The Athenians had been trying to supply the needs of God through their offerings. But actually it is he who supplies all their needs.

THE UNITY OF THE HUMAN RACE (17:26a)
Paul next affirmed that all races have come from a common stock: "From one man he made every nation of men, that they should inhabit the whole earth" (17:26a). Paul implied that through common ancestry all races are equal.

The Athenians had a different belief. They believed they had sprung from the soil of their native land, Attica. Actually, as F. F. Bruce points out, "They belonged to the earliest wave of Greek immigration into the land, so early that, unlike later arrivals, the Achaeans and Dorians, they had lost all memory of their immigration."[3] Because of this so-called superior ancestry, the Greeks considered themselves superior to non-Greeks, who were called barbarians.

But Paul would not tolerate such racism. Racism is sin,

and when preaching the gospel to racists we cannot ignore the wrongness of it. Actually, when a racist comes to Christ, one of the sins for which he must repent is his racism. Social sins such as racism, casteism, and class differentiation are transgressions against God's law as are personal sins such as intemperance, anger, and lust.

Paul's statement also reminds us that we must not pander to the prejudices and bigotry of our audience in order to win their favor. The Sinhala race in Sri Lanka has had a history of tension with the Tamil race. As a Sinhalese, I must never use ill will toward the Tamils to win a Sinhala audience. Neither can I use Sinhala exclusivism. I may delight in my racial heritage. But I cannot do so in a way that excludes any other race or implies that my race is superior to other races. This same principle applies also to white and black preachers. Black is beautiful. That needs to be affirmed. But white is beautiful too, for black and white are both creations of God and are equally important in his sight.

SOVEREIGN OVER THE NATIONS (17:26b)
Paul went on to give an amplification of this claim that God is Lord of the earth: "And he determined the times set for them and the exact places where they should live" (17:26b). He was proclaiming God's sovereignty over the nations. Some have understood the first of these two statements as referring to the seasons of the year (as in 14:17). But it is more likely that what Paul meant was "the divinely appointed periods for individual nations to flourish."[4] The powers that exert a wide influence on earth have been permitted to flourish by God. Today they may seem to be very powerful. But God has appointed a time when they will lose their power.

The evangelistic appeal of this affirmation is immense. When people are confronted with the claims of Christ, the first questions that come to their minds relate to the other forces that have been influencing them. They ask, "If I follow Christ, what will my friends think of me? Will they ridicule me? Will they reject me? How about my parents? Will they consider me unfaithful because I've forsaken the family religion? Will I be persecuted? Will I be a failure in business because I will have to give up my unscrupulous practices? Will I be a misfit in society? Will I jeopardize my prospects of marriage? Will I have to face reprisals from the national or local gods?" All these questions revolve around the issue of other forces that a person faces.

Indeed, other forces do exert some authority in this world. But the Christian need not fear them, for their authority is temporary. The eternal God holds final authority and all other forces are subject to his sovereign will. The most powerful system will one day fall. God has already determined that date. So it would be folly to bow down to or be afraid of any system that sets itself up as rival to God, be it religious, social, or economic. The only wise path to follow is the path of obedience to the sovereign Lord.

MAN SEEKING GOD (17:27)
Verse 27 has great significance for the study of the religions of man, and its implications will be explored further in chapter 8. Paul said that one reason for God acting upon creation in the way he had just described is "so that men should seek him and perhaps reach out for him and find him" (17:27a). Earlier we spoke of a thirst in every man for an experience of the supernatural. This thirst is partly caused by what man sees in creation, which gives him a sense of something, or rather Someone, beyond creation.

This sense of the supernatural causes man to "seek" God and try to "reach out for him."

Every witness would do well to take seriously what Paul said here. People are groping for the supernatural. They want to seek for something beyond themselves. This groping may take different forms, religious or secular, spiritual or material. We present the fulfillment of this quest of man, for the eternal God has revealed himself in Jesus Christ and opened the way for us to fulfill our inner quest for an eternal dimension.

Paul said that God "is not far from each one of us." The way to God is not through a great search for something hidden, for God is near.

THE HUMAN FAMILY AND THE FAMILY
OF THE REDEEMED(17:28)

Paul substantiated what he was saying by using two quotations from the Greek poets with whom his audience was familiar (17:28).

The first quotation, "For in him we live and move and have our being," has been attributed to Epimenides the Cretan. The statement proclaims man's dependence on God for his existence. The second quotation, "We are his offspring," has a very similar idea to the first. It is from a poem by Aratus about the Supreme Being of Stoic philosophy.[5] It proclaims that man derives his life from God.

The first impression one may get from these two statements is that Paul was describing God's relationship with his redeemed children. If so, the first quotation would imply that the Athenians were experiencing what Paul elsewhere calls the "in Christ" existence. The second quotation would mean that all men are children of God, born into the family of God of which Christ is the firstborn.

But this is not what Paul meant here. The preceding verses show that Paul was talking about the source of life in man. Verse 24 says God "made the world and everything in it." Paul was talking about a relationship God has with man because God is his Creator.

The Bible distinguishes between the human family of which God as Creator is Father in a general sense, and the family of the redeemed, of which God is Father in a particular sense. I have no problems about calling a Buddhist friend my brother because with him I belong to the human family. But I do not regard him as my brother in Christ.

In the first part of this speech, Paul spoke of the human family and its relationship with God (17:24-29). In the second part Paul showed how people in the human family can enter the family of the redeemed. They need to repent. If they don't repent, they will be judged (17:30, 31). In the first part we see God the Creator. In the second part we see God the Redeemer.

Creation and redemption are not synonymous. They are separated by three great acts: the fall of man, which cursed the human race; the work of Christ, which opened the door for redemption; and the faith of men and women, which appropriates this redemption.

NOTES

1. F. F. Bruce, *Paul: Apostle of the Heart Set Free* (Grand Rapids: Eerdmans, 1977), p. 240.

2. E. M. Blaiklock, *The Acts of the Apostles, The Tyndale New Testament Commentaries* (Grand Rapids: Eerdmans, 1959), p. 140.

3. F. F. Bruce, *The Acts of the Apostles: The Greek Text with Introduction and Commentary* (Grand Rapids: Eerdmans, 1952), p. 336.

4. I. Howard Marshall, *The Acts of the Apostles, The Tyndale New Testament Commentaries* (Grand Rapids: Eerdmans, 1980), p. 288.

5. Bruce, *Paul*, p. 242.

CHAPTER FIVE
THE SEVERE SIDE
OF THE GOSPEL

We have seen that in Paul's ministry in Athens he was not reluctant to dialogue with non-Christians and even agree with some of their religious teachings. We saw him using glimmerings of truth in their own poets to buttress his claims about the nature of God. But Paul never stopped with agreement. He went on to present a gospel that was so unique that he urged his hearers to leave their former ways of life to follow Christ.

THE FUTILITY OF IDOLATRY

In verse 29 Paul explicitly stated what he had been implying earlier: idolatry is wrong. In the previous verse he had said that we are God's offspring. Then he said, "Therefore since we are God's offspring, we should not think that the divine being is like gold or silver or stone—an image made by man's design and skill" (17:29). In the next verse he described idolatry as ignorance.

Paul had said that God is the very source of life. If so, how can he be represented by lifeless things such as gold, silver, and stone? Besides, how presumptuous it is for mortal man to think that he by his artistry can represent the eternal God!

Earlier we said that Paul was provoked by the sight of idols. But he did not show his anger outwardly. We pointed out that, even though Paul did not thunder against idolatry like the prophets, he did not condone it. He combatted it, using the method most appropriate for his audience. He argued against idolatry, using the force of reason. Paul showed no polite indifference to error. He was polite, but he exposed the folly and danger of the erroneous way of the Athenians. His commitment to truth and his concern for the Athenians required that of him. Paul accepted that these people were religious, but he showed that their religiousness was futile.

A Christian leader in Sri Lanka once said that when he saw the Buddhists worshiping at their temple, he discerned that the Holy Spirit was active in that worship, accepting and blessing it. Paul would recoil with horror if he knew that such a statement came from the lips of a Christian leader. Paul politely acknowledged non-Christian religionists. He did not have harsh words for them because they were ignorant of Christ's revelation. (I believe he would reserve such harsh words for Christian leaders like the one I've just cited!) Paul even used their religiousness as a stepping-stone in his presentation of the gospel. But he showed them that the form this religiousness took was wrong and that they should repent of it.

The method Paul used in his attack on idolatry is called persuasion. He used skillful argument to appeal to the minds of his hearers so that they would change their beliefs. In chapter 11 we will discuss the use of persuasion in evangelism.

A CALL TO REPENTANCE (17:30)

After arguing for the futility of idolatry, Paul urged his hearers to turn from it: "In the past God overlooked such ignorance, but now he commands all people everywhere to repent." After appealing to his hearers' minds with arguments against idolatry, Paul appealed to their wills, with a call to act on the truth and change the course of their lives.

Truth is important. But more important than that is what one does with the truth. Truth gives the basis upon which a person can act. But unless he acts on it, the basis is useless. In all our preaching our ultimate goal is to have the truth act upon the will. It is not enough to move people emotionally or have them give intellectual assent to what we say. Unless the effect travels from the emotions and the intellect to the will, there can be no lasting impact on the life.

Without repentance, then, there can be no conversion. This is why repentance is a key feature in the preaching of the Old Testament prophets, of John the Baptist, of Jesus, and of the apostles. Jesus begins his ministry in Galilee with the message, "The time has come. . . . The kingdom of God is near. Repent and believe the good news!" (Mark 1:15). After the first Christian evangelistic sermon of the early church, Peter exhorted, "Repent and be baptized, every one of you, in the name of Jesus Christ so that your sins may be forgiven" (Acts 2:38). A clear break from the past was called for, including baptism, which is a sign of incorporation into a new life and community.

There has been a tendency in recent times to focus so much on the need to accept the facts of the gospel that repentance has been downplayed. It has been associated with "works of righteousness." Some are even reluctant to ask people to make Christ their Lord when inviting them to receive his salvation. They say all one needs to do is to believe that Christ has died for his sins, to ask God to forgive him, and to accept the salvation Christ gives. Later we may preach on the lordship of Christ to those who have received his salvation. In extreme situations, lordship is even regarded as an optional extra for Christians. But the Bible does not separate the lordship of Christ from his saviorhood. When we receive him as Savior, we must also accept him as Lord. This dual call must be reflected in our preaching, too.

Many people are willing to "pray to receive Christ" into their lives when invited to do so. Yet this prayer may not represent a commitment of their lives to Christ. An Asian may respond to such an invitation out of politeness or purely because he thinks that it is the response expected of him by those who have hosted him for the Christian program he is attending. He feels like a stranger at the meeting. When the preacher asks him to raise his hand, he does it.

Others will try Jesus so that they can add on a dimension of fulfillment that is missing in their lives. People say the born-again experience enriches one's life. So why not try it? A Hindu might pray to receive Christ and add him to all his other gods. He will have pictures of Shiva, Krishna, and Jesus in his house and read devotionally from the Bhagavad Gita and the Bible. An unscrupulous businessman may accept Christ as his Savior but continue to underpay his workers and use other dishonest means for gain.

When one comes to Christ, he must leave behind all idols. Paul described the conversion of the Thessalonians thus: "You turned to God from idols to serve the living and true God" (1 Thessalonians 1:9). The idols in the person's life are those things that ultimately determine the decisions he makes. Say a person has been hurt by someone else and is contemplating how to respond to that hurt. He knows that God's Word says, "Love your enemies, do good to those who hate you" (Luke 6:27). But his hurt self says, "Retaliate; teach him a lesson; hurt him." If he obeys the self, then the self is his idol. When he repents he dies to his self, that part of him that chooses ways that oppose God's ways.

In Athens, Paul was calling for repentance from literal idols. If the Athenians were to come to Christ, they would have had to forsake Athenian religion. It is the same today. Some are saying today that one can be a Buddhist Christian or a Hindu Christian. That idea is alien to the Scriptures. You cannot serve Shiva and Christ, or Buddha and Christ.

Indeed, the convert to Christianity must retain many of the cultural distinctives of his upbringing. At one time Christians mistakenly regarded these as being opposed to Christianity. A young Sri Lankan Buddhist convert may delay his marriage by a few years so that he can save money to provide for his sister's marriage. This is a family obligation and becoming a Christian does not free him from it. He will buy gifts for his family members and celebrate the Sri Lankan New Year with them in April. (Christians in Sri Lanka mistakenly avoided this festival completely even though it had to do with the harvest and was not essentially a religious festival.) But our young convert will not participate in the religious ritual associated with the New Year festivities. Those rituals contradict his belief in the sovereignty of God over the forces of nature. He should pray to God regarding his crops and his needs. This could be done on New Year's Day instead of participating in these rituals that are an attempt to persuade other gods and forces to send blessings on him.

So this young man will be baptized as an indication that he has discarded his former religious allegiance and has joined the Christian community. He is not a Buddhist Christian. He is a Sri Lankan Christian. Unfortunately, many Christians in Sri Lanka are more like English Christians than Sri Lankan Christians. That must change.

People can have nonreligious idols too. One person's idol may relate to personal morality. When he comes to Christ, he resolves, and seeks God's help, to forsake his immoral actions. Another person's idol may be materialism. He has been ignoring some important principles in his quest for wealth. When he comes to Christ, he will need to give up some of his practices, such as accepting bribes. Another person's idol may be racism. When he comes to Christ, he gives up those things he had been doing that harmed those of another race, supposedly for the welfare of his own race.

Ultimately, however, repentance is turning from our own way to God's way. The evidences that we are going our own way are manifested in religious, moral, material, or social spheres. We must repent specifically of these sins, for until repentance gets down to the specifics, it is not repentance. But our basic sin is that we choose our own way rather than God's. When we repent we say to God that we hand over to him the reins of our lives. We do what he wants us to do, not what we want to do.

THE GOSPEL COMMAND (17:30)
It is significant that the call to repentance comes as a command. Paul said, "[God] commands all people everywhere to repent" (17:30b). We don't simply announce good news. We don't only invite people to accept Christ. We communicate a command to his subjects by the Lord of the universe. The gospel is good news to accept. But it is also a

command to obey. So Paul said that those who "do not . . . obey the gospel of our Lord Jesus" will be punished (2 Thessalonians 1:8).

Because of the command of the gospel, we can go out with a sense of authority and confidence. We are Christ's ambassadors who implore people on Christ's behalf to be reconciled to God (2 Corinthians 5:20). We do not need to apologize for sharing the gospel. We go with all politeness. We follow the proper protocol of the area in which we are witnessing. We respect the people, their customs, and their authorities. But we go with confidence, for we are representatives of the Lord of the universe.

The command of God extends to "all people everywhere." That is as comprehensive as one can get, so the church needs to take the gospel everywhere to everyone. Every person we meet needs to repent and turn to God. We often hear people say that we must not try to convert everybody. But our mission is not to help the Buddhist to be a better Buddhist. Such an attitude is completely contradictory to the revelation of God in the Scriptures. The devout Jew, Paul, who had advanced much in his religion, needed to give it up to follow Christ. He said that "all people everywhere" are commanded to repent. That includes the devout Buddhist, Muslim, Hindu, and the moral humanist. All of them come under the all-encompassing circle Paul drew around the whole human race when he said that God "commands all people everywhere to repent." All need to turn to Christ.

A WARNING ABOUT JUDGMENT (17:31)

Paul gave a warning to support his call to repentance: "For he has set a day when he will judge the world with justice by the man he has appointed." Receiving a new life is not the only result of repentance. One who repents also escapes punishment at the judgment. Every person must face God's judgment one day. The writer of Hebrews stated that "man is destined to die once, and after that to face judgment" (Hebrews 9:27).

Many people today do not like to be confronted with the fact of judgment. Many are hesitant to talk about it. It appears to be in bad taste to bring up in a conversation such an unpleasant topic. Yet evangelism without the message of judgment is not biblical evangelism. When we leave it out, we fail to give the whole message that God entrusted to us to take to the world.

If all that the Bible says about judgment is true, it would be strange for us not to talk about it. If a meteorologist knows about an impending cyclone, he must inform the fishermen who go out to sea. If he fails to do so, and they go out to sea and lose their lives, the meteorologist would be guilty of criminal negligence. The fisherman may not like to hear these warnings, but he must warn them, whether they like it or not.

It is the same with the message of judgment. It is a mystery that many who accept the principle of warning people about danger in everyday life do not extend this principle to eternal realities. Some fail to warn of coming judgment because they don't believe in the reality of it. Others are silent because they are not sure about it. But judgment is too serious an issue to remain agnostic about. They must, as soon as possible, make every effort to find out the truth. Some are silent even though they accept the reality of judgment, as they consider it too unpleasant an issue to talk about. Such selfish negligence is inexcusable (see Ezekiel 3:17-21).

F. F. Bruce reminds us that "Greek thought had no room for such an eschatological judgment as the biblical revelation announces."[1] The majority of Paul's sophisticated listeners in Athens would have scoffed at what Paul said about judgment. But that did not deter Paul. Many say that this type of "unpleasant" doctrine is best introduced after a person commits himself to Christ. But judgment is part of the essential New Testament gospel. The writer of Hebrews lists it among the "elementary teachings about Christ" (6:1, 2).

We must preach about love, which is the bright side of the gospel. Love, I believe, should be the primary focus of our evangelistic preaching. But we must not neglect to warn people about the coming wrath. This, along with the call to repentance, constitutes the severe side of the gospel.

At times there has appeared in the church some preaching about judgment that has given sensitive Christians legitimate grounds for embarrassment. These preachers give the impression that they are delighted at the prospect of people being cast into hell. But such misuse of the doctrine does not warrant disuse. John Stott says that we must be "clear and dogmatic . . . that hell is an awful, eternal reality." He adds, "It is not dogmatism that is unbecoming in speaking about the fact of hell; it is glibness and frivolity."[2] Some have said we must not frighten people into accepting the gospel. I would agree that fear should not be the only motive that brings a person to Christ. But it can be one of them. Fear can be what arrests a person to stop and consider the gospel. After his attention has been won, we can give him the fuller gospel.

A statement of Jonathan Edwards, whose preaching on wrath has been greatly misunderstood and misrepresented, is appropriate here. He said that some think it is an objectionable thing "to fright persons to heaven, but I think it is a reasonable thing to fright persons away from hell."[3]

Some say that they will not preach about hell without tears in their eyes. Indeed, there should be sorrow in our hearts when we contemplate the fate of the lost. But this is something we must have all the time. Paul constantly had "great sorrow and unceasing anguish in [his] heart" as he thought about the lostness of the people of his own race (Romans 9:1-3). We should desire to have such an attitude too.

But our inability to weep must not deter us from preaching about hell. If, when the meteorologist came to know about the coming cyclone, he was in the wrong frame of mind to communicate the message to the fishermen, he would still proceed with the communication. If he had waited to get into the right mood he may have been too late. In the same way, we too must earnestly seek the right attitude to preach about judgment. But because of the seriousness of the situation we can't be holding back this message saying our attitude is not right.

I must add that I do not believe the right attitude necessitates that we weep every time we preach about hell. Some people would do that. But that would be unnatural to some personalities. The need is not weeping, but urgency, a love that drives us to proclaim the message faithfully (2 Corinthians 5:14).

Paul urged us to consider "the kindness and sternness of God" (Romans 11:22). This combination of kindness and sternness must characterize all gospel preaching. The German New Testament scholar, Joachim Jeremias, in a book on the parables of Christ, talks of "the twofold issue of all preaching of the gospel." He describes this as "the offer of mercy and the threat of impending judgment inseparable from it, deliverance and fear, salvation and destruction, life and death."[4] May we too reflect this biblical combination of "the twofold issue" in our presentation of the gospel to non-Christians!

NOTES

1. F. F. Bruce, *The Book of Acts, The New International Commentary on the New Testament* (Grand Rapids: Eerdmans, 1954), p. 361.

2. John R. W. Stott, "The Biblical Basis of Evangelism," in *Let the Earth Hear His Voice,* ed. J.D. Douglas (Minneapolis: World Wide Publications, 1975), p. 76.

3. Cited in Leslie Woodson, *What the Bible Says about Hell* (1973; reprint, Grand Rapids: Baker, 1976), p. 76.

4. Ibid., p. 91.

CHAPTER SIX
THE SUPREMACY OF CHRIST

The most important part of any evangelistic effort is the presentation of Christ. He is the central message we have to proclaim to the world. The old saying, "Christianity is Christ," is still true. At the climax of his message at Athens, Paul made a clear presentation of the person and work of Christ. In evangelism, we are not ultimately proclaiming a set of principles but a person, Jesus Christ. We are calling on people to accept him as Savior and follow him as Lord.

Dr. E. Stanley Jones often gave evangelistic lectures to Hindu audiences in India, having Hindus as chairmen of the meetings. One such chairman, who was chief minister of a state, during his opening introduction said, "I shall reserve my remarks for the close of the address, for no matter what the speaker says, I will find parallel things in our own sacred books." At the close of the meeting he was at a loss for words. Dr. Jones had not presented "things"; he had presented a person, Jesus Christ; and that person was not found in their sacred books.[1]

THE MAN, JESUS

Paul said that God "will judge the world with justice by the man he has appointed" (Acts 17:31a). What is so special about this man? What distinguishes him from the founders of other religions? To answer these questions we must examine the following evidence: (1) his claims, (2) his spotless life, (3) his resurrection, and (4) the new life he gives.

HIS UNIQUE CLAIMS

Some of the most obvious considerations, when thinking about the supremacy of Christ, are the claims he made about himself. Other teachers said they were telling the truth. Christ said, "I . . . am the truth" (John 14:6). Other teachers asked people to follow their teachings. Christ asked people to follow him. More than twenty times in the Gospels Jesus spoke about the need to follow him. The other great leaders taught people to worship God. The Buddha and Muhammad would have recoiled at the idea of people worshiping them. Jesus accepted the worship of Thomas (John 20:28). Jesus made statements that clearly implied that he was God, and some of his hearers were so scandalized by these remarks that twice they wanted to stone him for blasphemy (John 8:54-59; 10:30, 31).

Seven "I am" statements appear in John's Gospel, showing that Christ claimed to be the source of eternal life. He said, "I am the bread of life" (6:35); "I am the light of the world" (8:12); "I am the gate" (10:7, 9); "I am the good shepherd" (10:11); "I am the resurrection and the life" (11:25); "I am the way and the truth and the life" (14:6); "I am the true vine" (15:1). Leon Morris reminds us that "in each case the Greek form of 'I am' is emphatic." Each saying includes the personal pronoun "I." "There is no need to include the personal pronoun unless emphasis is re-

quired." Morris concludes that to Jewish ears, the words
I am "aroused associations of the divine."[2] These and
other statements of Christ make us agree with J. T. Seamands' statement that the uniqueness of Christ "is not
something we *concede* to Christ, but something he *con-
fronts* us with."[3]

HIS SPOTLESS LIFE

What can we do with the claims of Christ? If they are true,
we must take them seriously and act upon them. But if
they are not true, Jesus must have been a deceiving liar,
or one suffering from delusions of grandeur, or one
mentally deranged. But looking at this spotless, loving life,
it is impossible to come to such a conclusion. Even non-
Christians accept Christ as the example of a spotless life.
Mahatma Gandhi said,

The gentle figure of Christ, so patient, so kind, so loving, so full of
forgiveness that he taught his followers not to retaliate when
abused or struck but to turn the other cheek—it was a beautiful
example, I thought, of the perfect man.[4]

But Gandhi refused to accept the absolute uniqueness
of Christ. Instead he held to the equality of all religions. But
the person who accepts Christ's life as that of a genuine
example to the world must also accept the thrust of his
teaching.

The uniqueness of Christ does not emerge from a few of
his isolated statements. It is a recurring theme that is foundational to his teaching. We may disagree with many statements made by a good person and still accept him as a
good person. But here is a case of the best man that ever
lived making certain startling statements about himself so
consistently that we cannot consider him apart from those

statements. To say Jesus was good is to accept the core of his teaching about who he is as good. His life and his statements about his uniqueness are too closely linked to be separated from each other.

A friend of mine in Sri Lanka, a retired school teacher, was reared as a Buddhist. He was a voracious reader, and one day he borrowed a book on the life of Christ from the public library in his hometown. On reading it he concluded that the life of Christ is unparalleled in human history. He knew a response was required of him. He could not simply admire Christ. He had to yield to his lordship. He became a Christian.

HIS RESURRECTION AS PROOF

One piece of evidence for the uniqueness of Christ is even more convincing than his spotless life. Paul said that Christ's resurrection provides the "proof" of Christianity. The concluding statement of Paul's Athenian address was, "He has given proof of this to all men by raising him from the dead" (17:31b).

Going through the speeches of Acts, George E. Ladd wrote: "The resurrection was the primary message of the earliest Christians." Ladd calls the Resurrection "the cornerstone of the entire New Testament."[5] We will not attempt to give the evidences for the fact of the Resurrection here, something that has been ably done in numerous books. Instead, we will show how the Resurrection attests to the uniqueness of Christ by validating his plan of salvation. Because he rose from the dead we can say that he is who he claimed to be and that he can do what he claimed to be able to do. Paul wrote: "[He] was declared with power to be the Son of God by his resurrection from the dead" (Romans 1:4). In Peter's speech on the Day of Pentecost, he clearly established the fact that Christ's death and resurrection qualify him to be Lord (Acts 2:32-36).

What is the link between Christ's resurrection and his lordship? The link is twofold. The first link is, as we have implied, that it attests to the stupendous claims that Christ made about himself. The most startling of these claims was that he would rise from the dead. If that is proved to be true, it also lends support to his other statements about himself, and what he had done. As Donald Guthrie put it, "The resurrection expresses God's satisfaction with what Christ has done. The exaltation of the person is the vindication of his mission."[6]

Second, the Resurrection tells us that Christ can be Lord of everything because, by rising from the dead, he defeated the forces that keep man from experiencing God's salvation. He conquered all of man's enemies and so is qualified to be Lord. The victory of Christ establishes his lordship.

He Overcame Sin. By rising from the dead Christ overcame sin. He said that he came to give his life as a ransom (Matthew 20:28; Mark 10:45). John the Baptist called him "the Lamb of God, who takes away the sin of the world" (John 1:29). How do we know he can do this? His death was supposed to be a ransom for our sins. How do we know his death is efficacious? He proved its efficacy by rising from the dead. Paul wrote: "If Christ has not been raised, your faith is futile; you are still in your sins" (1 Corinthians 15:17). The Resurrection won the victory over sin after the death paid the price for it. The Resurrection tells us that the sacrifice Christ offered for our sins will succeed in bringing us to God. As Paul said elsewhere, "He was delivered over to death for our sins and was raised to life for our justification" (Romans 4:25).

One feature of Christianity that many non-Christians find difficult to accept is the idea that Christ can pay the penalty for our sins. "How can one person die for another?" they ask. How do we know that through his death he is able to cancel the just consequences of our sins? The Resurrection tells us that the plan Christ initiated to save man did indeed work. It is proof that his sacrifice does pay for our sins. If Christ was able to overcome man's great enemy, sin, then he is qualified to be man's Lord.

He Overcame Death. When Christ rose from the dead, he also defeated another of man's great enemies—death. With all his scientific advancement, man has failed to conquer death. He may delay it, he may make it less painful, but death is still one of the most certain realities we face. Christ's conquest of death makes him the firstfruits of those who will be raised from the dead (1 Corinthians 15:20). This means that those who are one with him will also be raised as he was raised (1 Corinthians 15:21-23, 26). His resurrection has also freed us from the fear of death (Hebrews 2:14, 15). The fact that Christ has overcome this great enemy, death, also qualifies him to be the Lord of all men.

He Defeated Evil. Christ's rising from the dead assures us that evil has been defeated and that this defeat will be consummated in due course. When he rose from the dead he signaled the defeat of evil. Christ constantly spoke of the kingdom of God, saying that with his coming to earth he had inaugurated this kingdom. But he also spoke of the day when this kingdom would be consummated and all evil would be defeated. Paul's Epistles and the Book of Revelation explain this total conquest of evil in great detail.

Evil does have power in the world today, but it is limited

in scope and duration. The Resurrection started a process to defeat evil, a process that will end only with the total consummation (1 Corinthians 15:23-28). Terminology from the Second World War has been used to describe this process. Christ's work of death and resurrection (the Christ event) is compared to D day, when evil was dealt a decisive blow. Now what remains are the mopping up operations before the total victory (V-day). But that victory is sure because of what Christ has done.[7]

Many people wonder whether it is worth following Christ's way in this society where evil has so much power. For a non-Christian this decision is particularly costly. To follow Christ may mean persecution. He may think he will be threatened with reprisals from aggrieved deities whom he has discarded in order to follow Christ. The Resurrection assures us that it is worth making Christ our Lord. When Christ rose from the dead he not only defeated evil, he also ensured its final annihilation. In fact, we know that he uses the devices of the forces of evil to fulfill his own ultimate purposes (Acts 4:25-28). If this is so, the wisest thing for one to do is to join his side, for he is moving along a path that is headed for total victory.

The Resurrection attests Christ's lordship by showing that he is sovereign over our greatest enemies—sin, death, and evil.

THE GIFT OF A FULL LIFE
The Resurrection shows the supremacy of Christ in another way in that it helps us experience the "resurrection life" on earth. Through it we have the supreme experience, the only way to a complete life. The Resurrection is the means the Creator of life has provided for man to experience the purpose for which he was created.

Frees from Guilt. The resurrection life frees us from the guilt of sin. We have trusted in Christ for forgiveness and we know he will forgive us because when he rose from the dead he showed us that the sacrifice for our sins had been accepted (1 Corinthians 15:7). Paul wrote, "There is now no condemnation for those who are in Christ Jesus" (Romans 8:1).

Guilt is one of the most destructive forces in a person's life. It keeps sending the message, often to the subconscious, "You are no good." Psychologists have written volumes on how guilt feelings damage a person. Some of them say, "Don't add to a person's guilt by talking about sin." We, however, do talk about sin because we know the answer to guilt. We face up to the fact of our sinfulness and then let Christ cleanse us of our sin by his blood (Hebrews 10:22; 1 John 1:7). The great result of this is that God does not remember our sin any more (Jeremiah 31:34), freeing us from the burden of guilt.

When Paul thought on the facts of how God had mercy on the worst of sinners like himself, he spontaneously burst forth into a doxology: "Now to the King eternal, immortal, invisible, the only God, be honor and glory for ever and ever. Amen" (1 Timothy 1:17). Guilt has given way to gratitude; condemnation to adoration.

Becomes Our Friend. The Resurrection tells us that our Savior and Lord is alive. Since he is alive, he can be intimately related to us. Just before he left earth he said, "And surely I will be with you always, to the very end of the age" (Matthew 28:20). The fact of Christ's presence with us is a mystery to many non-Christians. My Buddhist friends in the university were quite amused at my description of God as my best friend. When I came to class in the morning, they would ask me whether I had talked to my best friend that day. I felt no hesitation to answer "Yes."

When a non-Christian comes to Christ, the fact that Christ is alive becomes one of the most joyous blessings of Christianity. He has begun to follow a living Lord. After a Muslim in Africa was converted to Christ, his friends asked him why he became a Christian. He answered, "Well, it's like this. Suppose you were going down the road, and suddenly the road forked in two directions, and you didn't know which way to go; and there at the fork were two men, one dead and one alive. Which one would you ask which way to go?"[8] The fact that Christ was alive attracted him to Christianity.

The Benefits of a Living Lord. The presence of Christ with the Christian has numerous benefits. Christ is like the Good Shepherd, guiding us through life, and he is sovereign over everything. This realization gives us a deep peace. It is most significant that when Christ met his disciples after he rose from the dead, he often gave them greetings of peace (Luke 24:36; John 20:19, 21, 26). This peace touches every area of life that could trouble us. We are freed from a troubled conscience that could bother us with guilt feelings over the past. We have courage to face the challenges of the present because Jesus, who is sovereign over all things, is with us. We are not anxious about the future. So the peace of Christ touches our attitude to the past, the present, and the future. It is a peace completely different from the peace the world gives (John 14:27), for it is not dependent on circumstances, but on him, and he is "the same yesterday and today and forever" (Hebrews 13:8).

We Have Resurrection Power. Because Christ is with us, we have available to us "the power of his resurrection"

(Philippians 3:10; Romans 6:4-7; Ephesians 1:19, 20). I was recently listening to a Buddhist talk over the radio and was impressed by how noble the Buddhist way of life is. In Buddhism there are many principles similar to the Christian ethical system. But I also realized that this noble path must be trod by the Buddhist in his own strength. We understand human nature well enough to know how impossible that is. Christ gives us strength to do what we must do. Paul said, "I can do everything through him who gives me strength" (Philippians 4:13).

The strength, or grace, Christ gives us is particularly important in the Christian way of salvation. Our salvation is not something we earn through hard work but something given to us as a gift. So, while other religions present different ways of life, Christ gives us the way to life. Christ said he came to give us "life . . . to the full" (John 10:10). Because of this, Christian living is a joyous response to God's working in us. It is not a losing battle for holiness, a dreary climb toward unreachable principles. It is the joyous experience of a full life, which the Creator of life himself has given us.

Here, then, is the fourfold base for our belief in the supremacy of Christ. First, he made some unique claims about himself that no other founder of a major religion made. Second, he backed these claims with a spotless life. Third, he attested these claims by rising from the dead. And fourth, he makes these claims real in our daily lives by giving us an experience of him that can only be described as life to the full.

CHRIST'S CLAIMS: NOT ABSOLUTE?
Some people reject the arguments for Christ's uniqueness presented here because they won't accept the first step in

our argument. They may agree that Christ lived a spotless life and rose from the dead and that he transforms people's lives. But, they say, the claims to uniqueness made about Christ must not be regarded as absolute and made to apply to the adherents of other religions.

Reasons for Rejecting Christ's Claims. Those who reject the absolute uniqueness of Christ's claims offer a number of arguments.[9] They say that these claims, which are attributed to Christ, are found mainly in the Gospel of John. They are not necessarily statements of Christ. They are expressions of faith in Christ and love for him of the Christians responsible for writing the New Testament. These Christians had a deeply fulfilling experience of Christ that is reflected in their writings about him. The uniqueness of Christ was a very precious reality to them. But this does not necessarily apply to non-Christians.

The claim that Christ is unique is said to be similar to the claim of a child that his father is the best daddy in the world. For this child this is an unmistakable reality. But the child next door would say the same thing about his father. This child, too, is articulating an unmistakable reality in his life. So, while we must respect the right of Christians to hold that Christ is unique, we must not convert such ideas into absolute truths that are binding on all people.

What, then, does one do with the statements claiming uniqueness that come from Christ's own lips in John's Gospel? They say that John's Gospel is essentially a theological document. Unlike the first three (Synoptic) Gospels, it is not historically reliable. Jesus' own teaching as seen in the Synoptic Gospels was theocentric, that is, centered in God. As the Christians became more aware of their uniqueness, especially their difference from Judaism, they became more and more Christocentric. As one writer put it, "Gradually Jesus comes to the centre and God is pushed to the periphery."[10] This shift is reflected in John's Gospel.

The faith and experience of the church told them Christ was unique. This belief, they say, is reflected in their descriptions of Christ. John's Gospel, being more interested in theology than history, is a prime example of this. In it Jesus was described as saying, "I and the Father are one" (John 10:30); and "I am the way and the truth and the life. No one comes to the Father except through me" (John 14:6). Objectors say that you will not find such claims in the Synoptic Gospels.

So these claims to uniqueness must not be regarded as coming directly from Christ. They are reflections of the faith and experience of the church found in John, which is a theological document not overly concerned with historical accuracy. Therefore, objectors claim, you must not raise these statements to the level of absolute truths and apply them to all people. They are true for Christians, but are not necessarily applicable to non-Christians.

John Is a Historical Document. A key to our response to the above argument is that we believe Christ did really make those statements about himself that are recorded in John. While we agree that John is essentially a theological document, we believe it is also a historically accurate document. While we agree that in John is reflected the faith and experience of the church, we believe that this faith and experience are based on historical truth. The early Christians said that Christ was unique not only because that was a truth that reflected their faith and experience, but also because that was a truth that Jesus literally proclaimed about himself.

The historical accuracy of the statements in John's Gos-

pel can be defended. However, one seeking a more de-
tailed defense should consult a specialist's treatment of the
topic.[11]

John appeared to be remarkably accurate on a number
of points. Examples are his accurate topographical references, his many references to Jewish feasts, and his pre-
cise notes of time, which show that he was interested in
presenting historical facts. When studying John's Gospel
we are struck not only by his theological intentions and
emphases but also by his profound respect for facts relating to Christ's life and ministry. He even claims to be an
eyewitness of the events he described (John 21:24). Donald Guthrie concludes, "His Gospel does not give the impression in its narrative of being other than a historical
account."[12]

The treatment of John the Baptist in this Gospel is a
highly theological one. We are not even told of John's bap-
tizing Jesus. The author's aim (as John 1:7, 8 shows) is to
demonstrate that John bore witness to Jesus (a theological
aim). The Qumram (or Dead Sea) Scrolls, coming from a
religious community living near the Dead Sea around the
first century, were discovered in the middle of the twentieth
century. The teachings found in these scrolls make points
of contact with almost everything that the Baptist said. To
biblical critics this is considered a gauge of accuracy.
These findings have helped convince such critics as J. A.
T. Robinson of the accuracy of the portrait of John the
Baptist in John's Gospel. Leon Morris comments: "If John
can be accurate when he is demonstrably concerned to
make a theological point, this creates a presumption that
he is accurate elsewhere." Morris asks, "If his portrait of
John is a good one, why should we think anything else
about his portrait of Jesus?"[13]

The noun and verb for "witness" appear forty-seven

times in John's Gospel, which is more than in any other New Testament book. *Witness* is a legal term used for what goes on in a court of law to establish the truth. Morris points out that "the use of this term shows that John's intention was to give facts and that he was confident that facts would stand up. There was adequate testimony behind what he said."[14]

Using this idea of witness, John built a strong case for the uniqueness of Christ. The Old Testament Scriptures, the miraculous signs, John the Baptist, and the disciples (especially Thomas) are all shown as bearing witness to Christ's supremacy.

John's Gospel also has more references to "truth" than any other New Testament book. Words such as *truth, truly,* and *true* appear more than fifty times in John. This unusual interest in what is true points to the conclusion that John was recording what really happened.

Some still say that John's idea of truth was different from ours, that he had no problem in including what did not happen under the idea of truth. Morris responds: "But this is conjecture. It must be proved; it is not enough to assert it. And it seems that the evidence is against it."[15] We conclude that the combined emphases on witness and truth argue powerfully for the fact that John intended us to take what he wrote as historically accurate.

It is generally agreed that the main purpose for the writing of John's Gospel was to combat Docetism, the heresy that Jesus had no contact with matter but only seemed to have such contact, that he was not a real man but simply appeared so. Against such an idea John proclaimed that the Word became flesh (John 1:14). He was concerned to show that Christ's birth, life, and suffering took place concretely in this material world. By writing a nonhistorical Gospel, John would have lost his case against the Docetists. He would be foolish to battle Docetism with anything other than historical evidence.

We know that the early church gave a high place to history. Firsthand contact with the historical Jesus was important for authenticating the gospel message. For example, the apostle chosen to take Judas' place had to have been with Jesus from the time of his baptism up to his ascension (Acts 1:21, 22). The First Epistle of John gives an indication of how important firsthand experience was in the early church: "That which was from the beginning, which we have heard, which we have seen with our eyes, which we have looked at and our hands have touched—this we proclaim concerning the Word of life" (1:1). Leon Morris observes:

What gave the peculiar quality to Christian faith was that the believers saw it securely rooted in historical events. They were not like Greeks or Romans, whose religions were replete with mythological stories that nobody credited. The Christians were not concerned with ideas, but with a Person. They maintained that that Person had lived and died and risen.[16]

The early Christians accepted John's Gospel and gave it a revered place in the Canon. They would not have done so if it was historically inaccurate.

Indeed, John is different from the Synoptics, but when John wrote he had in view a different audience and goal than did the authors of the Synoptics. The difference could be compared to two different accounts of a cricket game, which appeared a few days ago in one of our newspapers. One report was a general description of the game. The other report was more of an interpretive commentary, focusing mainly on the behavior of some of the players and how it affected the game. Both articles were accurate when it came to reporting facts. But their emphases were different. In the same way, because John had a different emphasis from the Synoptics, it does not mean it is factually any less accurate.

Our conclusion is that we cannot so easily dismiss the far-reaching implications of statements attributed to Christ by John. Because John is a historical document, these statements also reflect accurately what Christ said. Christ did claim to be unique and the only way of salvation for all men. That implies that other ways are inadequate as ways of salvation. Of course, we could ignore these claims, but we must not, because Christ authenticated them by his spotless life, his resurrection, and his transforming influence on people's lives.

Christ's claim to absolute uniqueness does not set well with those who are seeking a new type of "harmonious" relationship with other religions, which would necessitate the dropping of a call to conversion to Christ. Such people find very attractive the critical approach to John that denies its historicity. They are able to explain away the statements about Christ's uniqueness as arising from the experience of Christians and not from the lips of Christ. The trustworthiness of the Christian revelation is closely connected to the belief in the uniqueness of Christianity. Because these statements about his uniqueness are trustworthy, deriving from Christ himself, he is unique—absolutely unique.

Christ's Uniqueness in the Other Gospels. We must also dispute the claim that the Synoptic Gospels do not give as exclusive a picture of Christ as does John's Gospel. On the contrary, we see an equally clear presentation of Christ's uniqueness there. If the "I am" statements present Christ's supremacy in John, the "Son of man" statements present it in the Synoptics. As George E. Ladd has shown, "Son of man," in the time of Jesus, was "a messianic title for a preexistent heavenly being who comes to earth with the glorious Kingdom of God."[17]

The Synoptics portray the Son of man as coming in great glory with clouds and angels (Matthew 16:27; 24:30). He will be sitting at the right hand of power (Mark 14:62), on his glorious throne (Matthew 19:28). When he appears, all the nations of the earth will mourn (Matthew 24:30). He will be the judge of the nations (Matthew 25:32). Those who acknowledge him before men will be acknowledged before God the Father in heaven (Matthew 10:32). Even though heaven and earth may pass away, Christ's words will not pass away (Matthew 24:35). The Son of man is Lord of the Sabbath (Matthew 12:8). He has authority on earth to forgive sin (Matthew 9:6). These passages show how the Christ of the Synoptics regarded himself, so we are not surprised to find him asking people to forsake everything and follow him, a theme repeated often in the Synoptic Gospels.

We have been told that statements such as "I and the Father are one" (John 10:30) do not appear in the Synoptics. But Matthew 11:27 is very similar to this statement. Here Jesus said, "All things have been committed to me by my Father. No one knows the Son except the Father, and no one knows the Father except the Son and those to whom the Son chooses to reveal him." Jesus went on to say in the next verse, "Come to me, all you who are weary and burdened, and I will give you rest."

In view of the above, it seems surprising that some writers claim that the Synoptics do not teach the uniqueness of Christ in the way that John's Gospel does. Our conclusion is that the whole New Testament presents Christ as absolute and unique, as the only way available to man for salvation. To deny this is to be untrue to the New Testament.

ABSOLUTE TRUTH DIVIDES

Returning to Paul's ministry in Athens, we observe a very significant reaction to Paul's speech: "When they heard about the resurrection of the dead, some of them sneered, but others said, 'We want to hear you again on this subject'" (Acts 17:32). Some accepted Paul's message; others rejected it, which happened wherever Paul preached the gospel. It is to be expected. Insipid principles may get away with no opposition. But absolute truth, with its presentation of a unique Savior and its call to conversion (repentance), will divide its audience. Some will accept the radical change demanded or seek to know more about it. Others will reject it.

Absolute truth demands a response. One accepts it, or seeks to get to know about it better so that a decision can be made for or against it. We must not be surprised if some object to the message of Christ. If all agree, it may be because we have presented an insipid message very distant from the life-transforming gospel of the Lord Jesus.

This understanding of the gospel as absolute truth, which demands a response and so divides people, is very alien to much of the religious thinking today. People today are calling for a harmony of religions, with each one learning from the other without trying to convert him. Our belief in the supremacy and uniqueness of Christ causes us to take a totally different view. We see Christ as the only way to salvation and we urge "all people everywhere to repent" of their former ways and to follow Christ as their only Savior and Lord.

NOTES

1. Cited in J. T. Seamands, *Tell It Well: Communicating the Gospel Across Cultures* (Kansas City: Beacon Hill Press, 1981), p. 60.

2. Leon Morris, *The Lord from Heaven* (Downers Grove, Ill.: InterVarsity Press, 1974), p. 96.

3. Seamands, *Tell It Well*, p. 61 (italics his).

4. M. M. Thomas, *The Acknowledged Christ of the Indian Renaissance* (London: SCM Press Ltd., 1969), p. 119.

5. George E. Ladd, *I Believe in the Resurrection of Jesus* (Grand Rapids: Eerdmans, 1975), p. 43.

6. Donald Guthrie, *New Testament Theology* (Downers Grove, Ill.: InterVarsity Press, 1974), p. 96.

7. Oscar Cullman, *Christ and Time,* trans. Floyd V. Filson (Philadelphia: The Westminster Press, 1964), p. 141.

8. Cited in Seamands, *Tell It Well,* p. 69.

9. This type of argument is seen in S. Wesley Ariarajah, *The Bible and People of Other Faiths* (Geneva: World Council of Churches, 1985).

10. Ariarajah, *Other Faiths,* p. 24.

11. For example, Leon Morris, *Studies in the Fourth Gospel* (Exeter: Paternoster Press, n.d.); *The Gospel According to John* (Grand Rapids: Eerdmans, 1971), pp. 40-56; "Gospel According to John," *International Standard Bible Encyclopedia,* vol. 2 rev. ed. (Grand Rapids: Eerdmans, 1982), pp. 1104-6; and Donald Guthrie, *New Testament Introduction* (Downers Grove, Ill.: InterVarsity Press, 1970), pp. 323-8.

12. Guthrie, *Introduction,* p. 328.

13. Morris, *Encyclopedia,* p. 1106.

14. Ibid.

15. Ibid.

16. Morris, *Fourth Gospel,* p. 96.

17. George E. Ladd, *A Theology of the New Testament* (Grand Rapids: Eerdmans, 1974), p. 149.

PART TWO

CHAPTER SEVEN
GETTING TO KNOW
OTHER RELIGIONS

In his speech to the Athenians, Paul quoted with approval from two non-Christian poets (Acts 17:28). What Paul did here has numerous important implications, some of which we will explore in this chapter.

QUOTING NON-CHRISTIAN AUTHORS
The first thing we need to point out is that even though Paul quoted two non-Christian philosophers, nowhere are we told that he accepted the whole religious system of their philosophies. Yet he saw "glimmerings of the truth" in these systems that could be used to buttress his case for Christianity.[1] His audience was familiar with these writers and accepted them as their own teachers. In this case Paul saw that he could use something they had said in the process of developing his case for the Christian gospel.

We, too, as F. F. Bruce points out, "may quote appropriate words from a well-known writer or speaker without committing ourselves to their total context or background of thought."[2] We may use the decrying of hypocrisy by secular musicians while arguing for the need for an authentic existence. On our way to proclaiming Christ's death as the price paid for man's sin, we may use the insistence that wrongdoing must be paid for, an idea found in most religions.

MEETING THEM AT THEIR HIGHEST

By affirming what is good in the Greek philosophers, Paul gave us another important principle about the Christian's attitude toward other faiths. In Stephen Neill's words, "We must endeavour to meet them at their highest."[3]

Neill contrasts this with the approach of the witness who cheaply scores points off the other faiths "by comparing the best he knows in his own faith with their weaknesses." There are those who try to present a case for Christianity by appealing to the failures of non-Christians. Christianity is presented as the answer to the awful behavior of non-Christians.

In 1983 there was an outbreak of violence in Sri Lanka in which many from the Buddhist majority had a hand. Some Christians were quick to use this as evidence for the bankruptcy of Buddhism. But as we began to get a clearer picture of what had happened, news began to emerge that Christians too had been involved in the violence. Their involvement was not as prominent as that of the Buddhists because the Christians are a small minority in Sri Lanka. Besides, if we use this line of argumentation, all the Buddhist has to do is to point to situations such as Nazi Germany. We may not identify the Nazis as Christians. But since they were church members, the non-Christians did. These so-called Christians definitely became instruments of wickedness.

The "savagery" of the non-Christian world was used in the past to motivate Christians to missionary involvement.

Today the non-Christians are using the same argument to appeal for missionary involvement in the so-called Christian West. The Buddhists believe that the moral restraint of Buddhism is the answer to the immorality found in the West. The Hindus believe the devotion of Hinduism is the answer to the materialism found in the West. The Muslims believe that the brotherhood of Islam is the answer to the racial prejudice found in the West.

We do not argue for the validity of Christianity by pointing to the wickedness other religions have caused. We argue for it by pointing to the ravages of sin. It is sin that has caused the miserable state of the human race and not primarily the religion of these sinners. Sin is found in Christian and non-Christian environments. Those born into a Christian background need to be saved from sin as much as those born into a non-Christian background.

All this shows how careful we must be about attacking other religions. We must show people how their faith is ineffective and will not save. Paul did this regarding idolatry in Athens. We too need to show the ineffectiveness of the ways people use in their quest for salvation, such as materialism, idolatry, other gods, and self-effort. But we also see that Paul did not regard his gospel preaching as a competitive debate that he must win by putting down his opposition by every possible means. Paul's desire was to proclaim the truth. If there was truth to be found anywhere in these other faiths, he was not afraid to affirm it. But Paul showed, as he did in Athens, that the highest truths in these religions did not go far enough. Paul knew that the truth residing in other faiths would not bring eternal salvation. For this, Christ is the only way.

It is because we believe in the supremacy of Christ that we are not afraid to affirm what is good in other faiths. Christ is in a class by himself. The founders of the other religions were men who explored the meaning of the divine. Christ was divinity incarnate. He said, "Anyone who has seen me has seen the Father" (John 14:9). He also said, "I am the way and the truth and the life. No one comes to the Father except through me" (John 14:6).

We have come to the Father through Christ and tasted life and truth. We know that nothing in this world can compare with that. Our security in him takes away our defensiveness so that we are not afraid to affirm what is good in the followers of other ways. But, because we know that Christ is the only way to salvation, we do all we can to bring those following other ways to Christ.

We are not surprised to find that Paul proceeded to present a different gospel from that of the Greek philosophers he quoted. When Paul came to the resurrection of Christ he lost most of his audience. But Paul would not compromise truth in order to keep his hearers agreeing with him.

SOME PITFALLS

Many Christians, while studying the goodness in other religions, have strayed from faithfulness to the gospel. A few generations after Paul there were Christian apologists who followed Paul's example of quoting from non-Christian writings but made two big errors in the process. First, when trying to accommodate themselves to their audience, they downplayed some of the "offensive" features of Christianity. Second, they accepted some features of the non-Christian religions that were incompatible with Christianity. They set out to contextualize the gospel, but ended up diluting it. They became syncretists, something that happens often today, too.

Others begin to study non-Christian religions without understanding the supremacy of Christ. During their studies they come to appreciate the good points in these religions so much that, after prolonged interaction with them, they come to feel that the non-Christian religions are on a par with Christianity. They end up surrendering the uniqueness of Christ.

Still others, who have not fully appreciated the supremacy of Christ, become timid in their witness. They try to be faithful to the revealed Word of God, but they are hesitant to proclaim Christ as the only way to salvation. They may perhaps agree that the way of Christ is the best way. But they don't have the confidence to boldly call non-Christians to make the costly step of forsaking their faiths in order to follow Christ. So their witness is timid—too timid to encourage the radical step of conversion.

Because of these deviations from the truth by Christians who have delved into other religions, the noble biblical practice of contextualization has fallen into disrepute. Some Christians have gone to the other extreme of advocating that we stay clear of the teachings of other religions altogether. We are advised to simply preach the gospel "the way it has always been done." Actually this way was also a contextualized version when, under the influence of some bold pioneers, it first emerged a few generations ago. But over the years it has acquired a hallowed place in the minds of some Christians as being the only biblical way to do it.

An example of this kind of thinking can been seen in the way the King James Version is reverenced by some people. About 375 years ago, the King James Version appeared. For more than fifteen centuries before its appearance, other versions of Scripture had existed, the gospel had been preached, and people had received Christ. Yet today some seem to think that the King James Version is the only acceptable translation, as if it had always been so, and as if no other translation could be an improvement upon it.

We are told that to adapt our presentation of the gospel to our audiences is to compromise. If we preach the "plain and simple" gospel, people will come to Christ because of the power of the gospel and the sovereignty of God.

These critics of contextualization cite examples of people from a completely non-Christian background who were instantly transformed through a "simple" gospel presentation. I can attest to many such conversions and praise God for them. But we would do wrong to take these isolated instances and make a rule out of them. It is clear that the witnesses of the Bible, including Jesus the Supreme Witness, practiced the art of contextualization. If they did, so must we!

AVOIDING THE PITFALLS

Those who went astray didn't make the mistake of not interacting with other faiths. Their mistake was that while doing so, they neglected some of the necessary disciplines of the Christian life. When a soldier is at the battlefront, he has to be careful to maintain certain disciplines or he may get himself killed. These disciplines, such as alertness and sticking to the rules of personal safety, are useful in ordinary life, too. But they become critical at the battlefront. In the same way, those who dare to get out of the protection of the "Christian ghetto" so as to identify with non-Christians need to be especially alert to the kinds of disciplines all Christians should observe.

Three of these disciplines, which we will discuss here, are the Scriptures, the Christian community, and the Great Commission.

The Scriptures. The first discipline we need to maintain is a constant, dynamic contact with the Word of God, the Bible.

At any one time, the most important influence in any Christian life should be God's Word. The Word becomes particularly important when we interact with the heights of non-Christian reasoning. Prolonged contact with such reasoning could cause us to imbibe features from them that contradict God's Word. There is a great gulf between the highest of man's thoughts and God's thoughts (Isaiah 55:8, 9). Because we are human, we may be influenced in the direction of man's thoughts rather than God's thoughts. Man's thoughts sometimes seem to fit in more naturally with the human mind than God's thoughts, so our human thinking needs to be constantly challenged by God's way of thinking, by his principles and values. We can only achieve this through regular and prolonged exposure to the Bible. The Scriptures need to be the atmosphere we live in. Charles Spurgeon describes this principle very vividly:

It is blessed to eat the very soul of the Bible, until at last you come to talk in Scriptural language, and your spirit is flavoured with the words of the Lord, so that your blood is *Bibline* and the very essence of the Bible flows from you.[4]

The only way to think biblically is through a daily diet of the Scriptures. This is the reason Paul told Timothy, while instructing him on how to respond to false teaching, that he must constantly nourish himself in the truths of the faith and of the good teaching (1 Timothy 4:6). The person who studies other religions must first of all be a student of the Bible. It is from the background and the foundation of his prolonged exposure to the Scriptures that he exposes himself to the teachings of other faiths.

We also said that our contact with the Word should be dynamic. Because the Word is living and active (Hebrews

4:12), its impact upon us should also be living and active. Our time with the Word is actually a conversation with God, a conversation to which we go with an open heart and mind, ready to hear a life-transforming message. We don't approach the Scriptures only as students desiring to acquire more facts. We approach them as hungry infants yearning for milk and as obedient servants seeking instructions on what to do. If this is the type of contact we have with the Scriptures, it will transform us, and our thoughts will come into line with God's thoughts.

If our thoughts were God's thoughts, we would see the uniqueness of Christ, because God's Word clearly proclaims it. We would also be faithful to the revelation of God in the process of our contextualizing. Our message may be presented in words and methods familiar to the non-Christian, but the message itself would spring entirely from the Scriptures. One of the clearest examples of this in the Bible is Paul's Athenian address which, as we have said, was clearly biblical even though Paul used the quotes and methods of non-Christian philosophers.

Are we surrendering our intellectual freedom by confining our thinking to the boundaries set by the Scriptures? No! The decision to confine ourselves to the Scriptures was a free choice we made. We had come to accept the fact that the Scriptures contain the truth, and anything that contradicts its affirmations is an untruth. Such a choice was not a blind, unreasonable decision, but one based on convincing evidence for the trustworthiness of Scripture, something beyond the scope of this book to demonstrate. Our decision to live within the confines of Scripture is a free choice we have made, a choice that we believe is the wisest thing we could have done.

The logic of this choice can be explained from nature. I have all the freedom to jump off a high cliff. But I respect the force of gravity and have decided that when it comes to jumping, I confine myself to the boundaries of wisdom suggested by the law of gravity. I know that jumping from more than a certain height would be harmful to me. I do not feel inhibited or under bondage because of these facts. There are more profitable things I can do than jumping off a cliff!

The choice is the same with the Scriptures. I have chosen to confine my thinking to the boundaries allowed by the Scriptures. But in the Scriptures are contained inexhaustible riches. The opportunities to think creatively within the boundaries set by Scripture are so vast that a creative person would have in it more than enough to explore as long as he lives.

Christian Community. The second discipline necessary for effective contextualizing is the discipline of Christian community. The contextualizer needs to be accountable to a body of believers. The community acts as a check to the excesses of a creative contextualizer. He may be so eager to identify with non-Christians that he adopts ideas that go beyond the boundaries set by the Scriptures. He may be so excited about an approach to an issue that he has become blinded to its dangers. Others in the community, who are not so emotionally attached to this idea as to be blinded by its dangers, could be the necessary check on the excesses of a creative innovator.

The church in Antioch is a model for us of the effectiveness of Christian community life in evangelism. This was a daringly creative community that trod paths that others had not dared to tread. Their actions paved the way for the missionary movement that, I believe, is the most exciting movement in the history of the human race.

We are told that in the Antioch church there were prophets and teachers who worked together (Acts 13:1). Prophets are radicals who propose bold, new ventures. Teachers are generally more conservative and emphasize unchanging, foundational truths. Both these types are needed for a community to be healthy. One is a corrective to the excesses of the other.

Often radicals have no patience with conservatives, so they become independent. But by doing so they miss out on the enrichment that comes from community life and so minimize the chances of a lastingly effective ministry. Sometimes conservatives are so cautious that they oppose any bold venture proposed by prophetic visionaries.

Radicals and conservatives can work together effectively if both are consciously aware that they are subject to the authority of God's Word and if both share a passionate mission orientation. Then, out of the combined input of both groups, a community will emerge that, while being faithful to God's eternal principles, will move forward into bold and exciting ventures for Christ.

The Great Commission. Implied in what we have just said is the third discipline necessary for contextualization—a continuing commitment to the Great Commission. Anyone delving into other faiths must always bear in mind that his supreme task is to seek to bring all men to Christ.

Witnessing is an essential ingredient of a Christian life. For this reason Christ, after his resurrection, kept emphasizing the call to go into all the world. Bishop Vedanayakam Azariah of India used to invite people who had just been baptized to place their hand on their head and say after him: "I am a baptized Christian; woe unto me if I preach not the gospel."[5] If a person is not actively involved in fulfilling the Great Commission, he is being disobedient to Christ. That is, he is in a backslidden state. It is dangerous for backsliders to be formulating the theology and methodology of the church.

The desire to write this book came to me about eleven years ago when I was a graduate student in a theological seminary. At that time I pushed this desire aside for two reasons. First, I felt I did not have enough experience with other faiths to write such a book. Second, knowing the way many who had approached this topic had ended with such disappointing results, I feared that I too would stray from faithfulness to God's revealed Word and mission.

Writing is always an awesome responsibility. I believe the fear of misleading people is always a healthy one for a writer. But this time, when I felt I needed to work on this project, I did not drop it because of fear. I believe one reason for this was that I was actively involved in the work of the Great Commission.

For nine years now I have been active in ministry that relates evangelistically with non-Christians. I have experienced the power of God at work in my life. I have known the thrill of being a bearer of the gospel of Christ. There is a sense in which much of the power of the gospel is activated when we launch out into bold ventures of Christian witness. The experience of this power takes away my shame about the "scandal" of the gospel (Romans 1:16) and it creates in me a desire to share this gospel with all people (Romans 1:14-16).

I have seen the joy of those who have come to Christ from other faiths. I know enough of the lives of non-Christians through personal contact to be convinced that their greatest need is the salvation that Jesus brings. Involvement in the work of evangelism has increased my love for non-Christians and also deepened my conviction about the uniqueness of Christ. For these reasons I was not afraid to delve into the topic of the Christian attitude to other faiths.

So, we do not need to fear interaction with other faiths if we approach it from a background of vital contact with God's Word, of open fellowship within a Christian community, and of active commitment to the Great Commission.

NOTES

1. I. Howard Marshall, *The Acts of the Apostles, The Tyndale New Testament Commentaries* (Grand Rapids: Eerdmans, 1980), p. 289.

2. F. F. Bruce, *First Century Faith* (Leicester: InterVarsity Press, 1977), p. 45.

3. Stephen Neill, *Crises of Belief* (London: Hodder and Stoughton, 1984), p. 32.

4. Ernest W. Bacon, *Spurgeon: Heir of the Puritans* (Grand Rapids: Eerdmans, 1967), p. 109.

5. Cited in John R. W. Stott, *Our Guilty Silence* (Downers Grove, Ill.: InterVarsity Press, 1967), p. 59.

CHAPTER EIGHT
SOURCES OF TRUTH

In the last chapter we said there are truths in other faiths that we could affirm even though we know these truths do not suffice to lead a person to salvation. This brings us to the question of the source of these truths. Can they be described as God's revelation in the same way that the Bible is?

THREE SOURCES OF TRUTH
The Scriptures teach that there are three sources of truth available to man apart from the Scriptures.

God's Original Revelation. The first source is God's original revelation to Adam, the first man. Paul said that from "one man he made every nation of men" (Acts 17:26; see also Romans 5:12-21). This implies that Adam was the father of the whole human race. The Scriptures teach that God had a warm personal relationship with Adam. This could only have been possible if God had revealed key truths about his nature to Adam.

Yet with the Fall, man's nature was corrupted and untruths entered his mind. Paul wrote: "[Man] exchanged the truth of God for a lie, and worshiped and served created things rather than the Creator" (Romans 1:25). So man's religion deteriorated.

Yet that original revelation given to Adam was not entirely lost by the human race. In man there remained what has been called *reminiscent knowledge.*[1] In this reminiscent knowledge there is found truth about God.

The idea of the deterioration or devolution of religion is not accepted today in many circles. Many people prefer to explain the history of religions in terms of evolution rather than devolution.

The evolutionary theory claims that religion is man's attempt to answer certain questions and challenges he faces. From the earliest times man needed to explain how the world, with all its complexity, came into being. Man felt insecure because of his inability to control nature, so he began to look for someone bigger than himself to whom he could go for protection and blessing. He needed to attribute the misfortunes he faced to some source. Gradually man "created" ghosts, spirits, demons, and gods to answer his questions. There were gods for different functions and protecting different localities. So polytheism emerged.

As societies advanced, the evolutionary theory holds, man realized that having a supreme ruler for a large area was politically more effective than having many local chiefs. So monarchies emerged. This idea of the supreme ruler was extended to the religious sphere, yielding the belief in a supreme god. The climax of this process was monotheism, the belief in *one* supreme god.

The Bible affirms the very opposite of the evolutionary view. The Bible states that the first man had a monotheistic belief in the supreme God that was corrupted after the Fall, resulting in polytheism and animism (spirit worship).

Carl F. H. Henry regards the evolutionary explanation of religious history as typical of the mood of this age. He says, "In every age philosophers have sought some one explanatory principle by which to encompass and explain all things." He points out that "in modern times that principle has been the category of evolution."[2] So the development of religion is also explained in terms of evolution.

Anthropological studies carried out in this century however have given convincing evidence for the biblical view, which sees the present religious diversity in terms of the deterioration of an original revelation. Don Richardson has made these insights from anthropology available from a nontechnical viewpoint in his book *Eternity in Their Hearts.* He shows how the idea of a supreme, good God was discovered in thousands of so-called primitive cultures that have been studied in this century.[3]

Richardson relates how these discoveries were embarrassing to many anthropologists because they went against current opinions about the history of religions. They had expected "unadvanced" thoughts about the divine. The so-called advanced concept of a supreme God was a most unexpected discovery because these primitive cultures were not considered to have evolved to the point of developing such an idea. Richardson reports that "probably 90 percent or more of the folk religions of this planet contain clear acknowledgment of the existence of one Supreme God."[4]

When missionaries go out and proclaim the gospel to these cultures, their hearers often automatically identify the Christian God with their supreme God, a fact that has simplified the Bible translator's task. Bishop Lesslie Newbigin notes that "in almost all cases where the Bible has been translated into languages of the non-Christian peoples of the world, the New Testament word *Theos* [Greek for

'God'] has been rendered by the name given by the non-Christian peoples to the One whom they worship as Supreme Being."[5] Newbigin cites the great Bible translations consultant, Eugene Nida, who has pointed out that where translators tried to evade the issue by simply transliterating the Greek or Hebrew word, the converts would explain this foreign word in the text of their Bibles by using the indigenous name for God.

Here then is the first source of truth in non-Christian systems—God's original revelation. Though this revelation has been corrupted because of sin, some truth still remains, and that truth may be affirmed and used as a stepping-stone in communicating the gospel.

The Image of God in Man. The second source of truth available, apart from the Scriptures, is the very nature of man. Man is a religious being. The Dutch theologian, J. H. Bavinck, points out that "this is not to say that every man has this religious trait to the same extent." Some are more religious than others. But if we look at the human race as a whole, we must agree with Bavinck that "it cannot be denied that religiousness is proper to man." Bavinck says, "Even when a man turns his back upon the religious traditions in which he has been brought up and calls himself an atheist, he still remains in the grasp of his religious predisposition. He can never wholly rid himself of it."[6]

Religions such as Buddhism deny the necessity of relating to any supernatural being. But most of the adherents of such religions cannot generally be made to stick to a rigid non-theism. Mahayana Buddhism is the largest branch of Buddhism. It is practiced in countries such as Japan, China, Korea, and Tibet. The Mahayana Buddhists worship the Buddha and the *Bodhisattvas* and address their prayers to them as they would to gods. Hinayana Buddhism is practiced in countries such as Sri Lanka, Burma, Thailand, and Cambodia. It prides itself in being closer to the teachings of the Buddha and the early Buddhist (Pali) scriptures. Yet Buddhists belonging to this branch have also included the divine factor into the practice of their religion. Many Buddhists of Sri Lanka have literally deified the Buddha, a practice he would have opposed. These Buddhists often talk about the gods who protect them. The morning newspaper on the day that I write this carries a statement by the leading executive officer of Sri Lanka's most prestigious temple. He says that the temple lands "are dedicated to the Buddha and the gods." These Buddhists often resort to assistance from the gods or spirits in times of trouble.

Communism sought to eradicate religion with its strong rationalistic and materialistic emphases. But today religion thrives in communist lands in spite of the discrimination and persecution that religious adherents have had to face.

The incurable religiosity of man is a vestige of the image of God in man (see Genesis 1:26, 27). This image was tarnished as a result of the Fall so that no part of man has escaped the taint and pollution of sin. But man still has some of the God-implanted characteristics and abilities originally invested in him. These traits manifest themselves in ways that are both good and bad, which is why man thirsts after the divine. Ecclesiastes 3:11 says that God has "set eternity in the hearts of men." That refers to the vestige of the image of God. But it goes on to say that men "cannot fathom what God has done from beginning to end," which is a result of the fall of man. What man knows about God because of his natural inclination toward the religious is termed by theologians "the *intuitional knowledge* of God."[7]

So we find that man can think reasonably. He has a sense of the reality of the divine that expresses itself in religiousness. He has a sense of truth, of beauty, and of goodness. He has the potential for creativity. He has a sense of the eternal, which makes him want to transcend his limits of time and space. These are qualities with the potential of being used in the service of truth for the benefit of man. But they may also be used in ways that are dangerous to man. So we find accomplished art, literature, and music that are good and we also find accomplished art, literature, and music that are evil. We have beautiful ancient buildings regarded as wonders of the world that were built using slaves in a most inhuman way.

A Christian, therefore, may enjoy the music of Ravi Shankar or be challenged by the heroism of Mahatma Gandhi. We may learn from the literature of Greece. We could say that, because these are expressions of the image of God in man, the good features in these creations are derived in some sense from God. But we also know that those who created them do not know God, and this makes us unwilling to endorse the system of life to which they subscribe. As a youth I used to follow Hindu processions for hours, thrilled by the music I heard, but deeply troubled by what caused the musicians to play what they played.

The Plan of the Universe. A third source of knowledge, outside the revelation of God in the Scriptures, is the plan of the universe. Looking at the universe, man is able to make inferences about the One who created it. We may call this the *inferential knowledge* of God. The Psalmist said, "The heavens declare the glory of God; the skies proclaim the work of his hands" (Psalm 19:1).

Paul explained this knowledge of God more clearly: "What may be known about God is plain to them, because God has made it plain to them. For since the creation of the world God's invisible qualities—his eternal power and divine nature—have been clearly seen, being understood from what has been made" (Romans 1:19, 20).

In his speeches in Lystra and Athens, Paul said that the plan of creation is a testimony to God, creating in man a desire to know more about him (Acts 14:17; 17:26, 27).

By observing the grandeur of creation, people may be led to acknowledge the greatness of the Creator. By observing the laws of nature, people may arrive at a conviction about the importance of order for a secure life. This in turn will become a base for formulating the laws of a given society.

GENERAL REVELATION AND SPECIAL REVELATION
The three sources of truth outside the Bible are: reminiscent knowledge, based on the original revelation of God; intuitional knowledge, which comes by the use of our natural instincts; and inferential knowledge, which comes by observing creation. In theology, this type of knowledge is described under the heading of *general revelation.* It is truth, derived from God and available to all people. It is distinguished from *special revelation,* which is truth communicated by God infallibly, in the form of language. This truth is recorded in the Bible. Whereas general revelation gives hints about the nature of reality, special revelation is a clear guide to all that is needed for salvation and for authentic living.

Psalm 19 describes these two sources of truth. Verses 1-6 describe general revelation. This revelation is not made through "speech or language" (v. 3). But "their voice goes out into all the earth" (v. 4). Verses 7-11 describe special revelation. This description begins with the words, "The law of the Lord is perfect" (v. 7). It goes on to describe this revelation as "trustworthy" (v. 7), "right," "radiant" (v. 8), "pure" and "altogether righteous" (v. 9). This passage also describes the amazingly complete influence it exerts on believers. We affirm that only the Bible can exert such infallible authority upon man. No other writing, Christian or non-Christian, is revelation in the sense that the Bible is.

Some recent works on the Christian attitude to other faiths have disputed the Christian claim to a unique revelation. One writer says, "What we have in the Bible are not attempts to project objective truths, but a struggle to understand, to celebrate, to witness, and to relate."[8] To that writer the Bible is an expression of the faith and experiences of its writers. We must not make claims that it presents "absolute and objective" truths based on our belief that it is a unique revelation given by God, he says, "for most religions like Islam and Hinduism, are also based on the concept of revelation; and throughout history different persons have claimed to have various revelations from God."[9] It is not within the scope of this book to defend our belief that the Scriptures are a unique revelation from God, containing objective and absolute truth. This has been adequately done in numerous books on revelation that have appeared recently.[10]

LEARNING FROM OTHER FAITHS?
If glimpses of truth are found in other faiths, then there may be times when Christians can learn from those other faiths. This can be explained in two ways.

First, even though the revelation of God is complete in that it gives all that is needed for salvation and authentic living, God has given us the privilege and responsibility of applying this revelation to our specific situations. In some areas, we have specific instructions that are absolutes, such as the prohibition of adultery. But in other areas, we have general principles. And it is our task to apply these principles to our specific cultural situations. An example of this is the principle of reverential worship. In applying this principle, we may learn much from the music used by the non-Christians in a given culture. Music has been called the language of the heart. By listening to non-Christian music, we may learn much about the type of music that is suitable for the people of the culture which we are considering.

Another way to learn from other faiths is a little more complex to explain. Even though God's revelation is complete, our perception of it is incomplete. So, we have a lot to learn. The Scriptures contain all that is necessary for a complete life, but because of our cultural conditioning, we may be hindered from learning some of the things clearly taught in the Scriptures. Other cultures may not have these cultural hindrances. So, even without the light of the gospel, people of other cultures may achieve heights in these areas simply by availing themselves of general revelation.

I have a dear friend, a convert from Hinduism, for whose spiritual nurture I have had some responsibility. As my relationship with him developed, I realized that there was much I could learn from him about meditation, devotion, and reverence in prayer. Many of us in Sri Lanka, who grew up in a Christian background, were weak in our understanding and practice of meditation, devotion, and reverence. I sensed that his Hindu background had contributed positively to the development of his Christian prayer life.

When my friend came to Christ, he understood the true nature of prayer. He saw that prayer is a personal conversation between a child and his loving Father. To him this was a new, revolutionary, and liberating truth. He knows now that the Hindu prayers, which he had offered in some sense as a means of salvation, had no saving value. He does not use prayer hoping that it will be a way to merit salvation. Prayer is now a consequence of the salvation that he received as a gift from God, an expression of an intimate relationship he has with God, who is now his loving Father.

Into this relationship with God he brought a meditative, devotional reverence that he had acquired from his Hindu background. This reverence had expressed itself in ways that were contrary to the gospel. But the reverence itself was a good feature. We could say that it had its roots in God's general revelation and, therefore, we could learn from it.

Reverence is advocated in the Bible, too. The second statement in the Lord's Prayer, "Hallowed be thy name," is evidence of this. But the Christian tradition in which I grew up was so rational in its approach to truth that it had lost some of the reverential character essential to Christianity. My Christian experience in that area was biblically defective. Asian religion had preserved this reverential aspect, partly because the Asian culture is not overly rational in character. So, even though we know that Hinduism is not a way to salvation, we can learn from the Hindus about reverence. We know, however, that the fullest revelation about reverence is found in the Scriptures, but we had been blinded from seeing it because of the defective Christianity we inherited.

A good example of the defectiveness in our Christianity emerges when we look at our attitude toward nature. The Psalms tell us that the creation is daily proclaiming truths about God (19:1-6). Yet most Christians do not seem attuned to these messages. In fact, we don't know how to listen to such a voice. To us, nature is something to be used for the benefit of man. We may perhaps use its greatness to argue for the existence of God, but beyond that, we hardly see it as a source of truth. We have lost the meditative or contemplative aspect of life.

I believe this deficiency is one reason why Christianity has made minimal inroads into the societies of Asia, where the religions with a high emphasis on the contemplative are practiced. Many Buddhists and Hindus, for example, have been unimpressed by Christianity. They view Christians as irreligious people because of our lack of emphasis on the meditative and contemplative aspects of life. This is unfortunate, because these two areas are clearly presented as important aspects of God's complete revelation to man.

UNACCEPTABLE SYSTEMS

Though we may accept and learn from certain practices in non-Christian systems, we must reject the systems themselves. We know that Hindu devotion does not lead to salvation, for only faith in Christ does that.

We must disagree with the syncretist who says, "Let us learn from each other and live harmoniously with each other. After all, we are headed in the same direction, even though some of our practices may differ." The biblical Christian says, "We are not headed in the same direction. Some of our practices may be similar. We may learn from each other, but there is a sense in which we cannot live harmoniously with each other. We seek to bring all who are outside of a relationship with Christ into such a relationship, and that necessitates the forsaking of their former religions."

The syncretist says that we are one in the center, though we may differ on some peripheral details. The biblical Christian says that, though we may have some peripheral similarities, we are different in the center. Christianity revolves on a different axis from other religions. The way of Christ leads to life. The Bible teaches that other ways lead to death.

We approach the issue of truth and goodness in other faiths from the basis of our belief in the uniqueness of Christ. If an aspect of a certain religion conforms to the complete revelation in Christ, we affirm it. But if it does not conform to this revelation, we reject it. As Lesslie Newbigin puts it: "Jesus is for the believer the source from whom his understanding of the totality of experience is drawn and therefore the criterion by which other ways of understanding are judged."[11] These are implications of Christ's proclamation that he is "the truth" (John 14:6).

The good points in a religion that have their base in general revelation, as we said, may be used by the Christian evangelist as points of contact and stepping-stones in preaching the gospel. But we need to add that these same good features in a religion can also lead people astray.

The noble ethic of Buddhism, with all its good features, gives many people the encouragement to try to save themselves. They feel satisfied that they are using their own efforts to win their salvation. But self-effort is the opposite of God's way of salvation, which is by faith. Before one exercises such faith he must first despair of his ability to save himself. The ethic of Buddhism may cause people to trust in their ability to save themselves and so blind them from the way of salvation. So, Satan can use the best in other faiths to lead people away from the truth (2 Corinthians 4:4).

COOPERATING IN COMMON CAUSES
Another implication of our belief in general revelation relates to our cooperation with non-Christians in moral, so-

cial, or political causes of mutual concern. Theologian John Jefferson Davis has given a rationale for such activity. He says that even unbelievers have a God-created conscience. Because of general revelation, believers and unbelievers can overlap in their moral concerns.[12] So we may cooperate with non-Christians in causes such as peace, ecological responsibility, social development, and opposition to abortion.

We must, however, be warned that such cooperation is fraught with numerous pitfalls. Davis says that one of the keys to avoiding problems is to define the basis of cooperation narrowly and specifically.[13] We cooperate on some agreed-upon causes and no more. Davis also says that we must ensure that the group that is formed has a clear written statement of goals that does not conflict with Scripture.

We must remember that our supreme task, evangelism with conversion in view, is repulsive to most non-Christians. Cooperation with non-Christians must not result in a blunting of our evangelistic emphasis. Sometimes evangelistic organizations downplay their evangelistic emphasis so as to get assistance from the government or a non-Christian foundation for some social venture. This practice can be very dangerous. We must make known the fact that along with our social concern is an evangelistic concern, which we will not drop in order to get funds. Because they refused to hire homosexuals on their staff team, the Salvation Army in New York recently forfeited large sums of state assistance.

Following the recent racial riots in Sri Lanka, I participated happily in a neighborhood peace committee chaired by a Buddhist and of which most of the members were Buddhists. I found that what I did in that committee did not conflict with my Christian principles. But I could not participate in some ventures organized by certain Christians, such as an ecumenical rally at which the chief speaker was a Buddhist chief priest. I felt I couldn't take part because true Christian ecumenicity cannot extend to other religions. I also could not participate in many united services of prayer for peace that were held all over the land in Christian church buildings. At these services Hindus and Muslims joined with the Christians and offered Hindu and Muslim prayers for peace in the land along with Christian prayers.

These ecumenical rallies and united prayer services were hailed as great steps forward in the quest for interreligious understanding and harmony. But a biblical Christian, in his search for harmony with others, cannot surrender the scriptural teaching about Christ's uniqueness. Paul stated very clearly that the only acceptable way to God in prayer is through the mediation of Christ (1 Timothy 2:1-8). A Christian, therefore, cannot have a "united" prayer service where both Christian and non-Christian prayers are offered.

Murray Harris described the principle Paul laid down in his famous passage about being unequally yoked with unbelievers (2 Corinthians 6:14-16):

Do not form any relationship, whether temporary or permanent, with unbelievers that would lead to a compromise of Christian standards or jeopardize consistency of Christian witness. And why such separation? Because the unbeliever does not share the Christian's standards, sympathies, or goals.[14]

NOTES

1. Bruce A. Demarest, *General Revelation* (Grand Rapids: Zondervan, 1982), pp. 227, 228.

2. Carl. F. H. Henry, *God, Revelation and Authority: God Who Speaks and Shows,* vol. 1 (Waco: Word Books, 1976), p. 401.

3. Don Richardson, *Eternity in Their Hearts* (Ventura, Calif.: Regal Books, (1981), chapter 1.

4. Ibid., p. 44.

5. Lesslie Newbigin, *The Open Secret* (Grand Rapids: Eerdmans, 1978), p. 192.

6. J. H. Bavinck, *The Church Between Temple and Mosque* (reprint, Grand Rapids: Eerdmans, 1981), p. 15, 16.

7. Demarest, *General Revelation*, p. 228.

8. S. Welsey Ariarajah, *The Bible and People of Other Faiths* (Geneva: World Council of Churches, 1985), p. 27.

9. Ibid, p. 28.

10. Leon Morris, *I Believe in Revelation* (Grand Rapids: Eerdmans, 1976) is an excellent nontechnical study. Carl F. H. Henry's monumental *God, Revelation and Authority,* vols. I-IV, *God Who Speaks and Shows* (Waco: Word Books, 1976-1979) deals with almost every conceivable issue related to the doctrine of revelation. See also Carl F. H. Henry, ed., *Revelation and the Bible* (Grand Rapids: Baker Book House, 1959); J. I. Packer, *"Fundamentalism" and the Word of God* (Grand Rapids: Eerdmans, 1958); Bernard Ramm, *Special Revelation and the Word of God* (Grand Rapids: Eerdmans, 1961).

11. Newbigin, *Open Secret,* p. 191.

12. Cited by Randy Frame in *Eternity,* Jan. 1985, pp. 19, 20.

13. Ibid., p. 21.

14. Murray J. Harris, "2 Corinthians," *The Expositor's Bible Commentary,* vol. 10 (Grand Rapids: Zondervan, 1976), p. 359.

CHAPTER NINE
THOSE WHO HAVE NOT HEARD

One of the key affirmations of this book has been that Christ is supreme over all other lords and systems that claim the allegiance of men and women. We have shown that the truths in other religions do not suffice to mediate salvation to their adherents. Now we come to the crucial question of the destiny of those who do not receive Christ's lordship, especially of those who have not heard his gospel.

ONE WAY TO SALVATION

The Bible very clearly teaches that Christ is the only way to salvation. Jesus said, "I am the way and the truth and the life. No one comes to the Father except through me" (John 14:6). Peter told the Jewish leaders, who were very unwilling to accept the supremacy of Christ, "Salvation is found in no one else, for there is no other name under heaven given to men by which we must be saved" (Acts 4:12).

The salvation Christ offers is appropriated through faith in him. So, when the Philippian jailor asked Paul and Silas, "What must I do to be saved?" they responded, "Believe in the Lord Jesus, and you will be saved" (Acts 16:30, 31). Acts 2:21 and Romans 10:13 summarize this teaching by proclaiming that "Everyone who calls on the name of the Lord will be saved."

But what of those who have never heard? Will they be punished for rejecting a gospel they know nothing about? If so, God would be very unfair. The Bible does not teach that they are lost because they reject the gospel. Rather, it says that people will be judged according to their response to the light they have received. But it also shows that no one lives according to the light he receives, and that no one can be saved without the gospel. Paul explained this truth in Romans 1–3.

LIGHT THROUGH CREATION (ROMANS 1:19-25)
While developing his case, Paul often touched on the topic of the light available to people apart from the gospel of Christ. He saw light as coming through creation, through the conscience, and through the law of Moses. Paul's comments on the first two of these sources of light are of great significance.

Paul began a new section of his letter with an affirmation that "the wrath of God is being revealed from heaven against all the godlessness and wickedness of men" (1:18). This wickedness, he said, caused men to "suppress the truth," and that the truth they suppress is the truth about God that is revealed in creation:

What may be known about God is plain to them, because God has made it plain to them. For since the creation of the world God's invisible qualities—his eternal power and divine nature—have been clearly seen, being understood from what has been made (Romans 1:19, 20).

As C. K. Barrett explains, Paul was saying that by observing the creation man should arrive at the conclusion that "creation does not provide the key to its own existence."[1] From creation man should realize that there is a God beyond creation.

Men are held accountable to make an appropriate response to this message that comes from creation. Paul showed that because of this knowledge "they are without excuse" (1:20). C. E. B. Cranfield explains Paul's argument this way: "[Men] have been constantly surrounded on all sides by, and have possessed within their own selves, the evidence of God's eternal power and divinity, but they have not allowed themselves to be led by them to a recognition of him."[2] Paul said that God may rightly visit them with wrath (1:18) because, "though they have not had the advantage of hearing the gospel, they have rejected that rudimentary knowledge of God which was open to them."[3]

Paul described how man rejected the knowledge of God available to him: "For although they knew God, they neither glorified him . . . nor gave thanks to him" (v. 21). Their problem was not the lack of knowledge. It was rebellion. The next step in man's descent away from God was idolatry. They "exchanged the glory of the immortal God for images made to look like mortal man and birds and animals and reptiles" (v. 23). Paul concluded, "They exchanged the truth of God for a lie, and worshiped and served created things rather than the Creator—who is forever praised" (1:25).

Paul affirmed that all men have the opportunity to respond to God through the light they receive from creation, but they reject this light and choose their own religious practices (1:18-21). This is because they were not willing to glorify God as God or give thanks to him (1:21). They chose to go their way rather than God's way, which is the basic sin of man—independence from God. Because of it, all men in their natural state are under God's wrath (1:18).

LIGHT THROUGH CONSCIENCE (ROMANS 2:12-16)
Paul said, "All who sin apart from the law will also perish apart from the law" (Romans 2:12). Paul mentioned specifically those who have not come under the influence of God's special revelation. They will not be judged for the failure to keep a law of which they know nothing. The principle Paul was laying down here is, in the words of F. F. Bruce, "that men are judged by the light that is available to them, not by light that is not available."[4] The Gentile, however, does not live according to this light. He sins and he will be judged accordingly.

What is the light that is available to the Gentile? Earlier Paul had mentioned the light coming from creation. Later he mentioned the light from conscience, "They show that the requirements of the law are written on their hearts, their consciences also bearing witness, and their thoughts now accusing, now even defending them" (2:15). There is a sense of right and wrong that all people experience through the operation of their consciences. Because of its operation on a person's will, the conscience of each individual one day will accuse or defend him. This accusing and defending "will take place on the day when God will judge men's secrets through Jesus Christ" (2:16). So the Gentiles will be judged according to what they did with their consciences.

The conscience may even defend Gentiles at the judgment (2:16). Some have taken this verse to mean that there are those who will stand before the judgment and be acquitted, even though they did not know Christ, because they were faithful to the voice of their conscience. But this is not what this passage says. Paul was saying that at the judgment some of the actions of people will be shown to be faithful to their consciences whereas other actions will be shown to be in opposition to their consciences. Later on in this chapter we will show that people's good and bad actions will significantly influence the judgment they will receive. But that is not the whole story. As Max Warren points out, "Paul's argument does not end at Romans 2:16." Paul went on the show that "man's conscience is in greater or lesser degree sadly distorted."[5] Paul later described the whole human race, without exception, as under sin, lost, and in need of a supernatural work of grace for salvation.

ALL UNDER SIN (ROMANS 3:9-12, 23)

Paul made an extended defense of the fact that all men in their natural state cannot be regarded as righteous before God because of their sin (1:18ff.). He summarized his case by saying, "What shall we conclude then? Are we any better? Not at all! We have already made the charge that Jews and Gentiles alike are all under sin" (3:9). He then amplified:

As it is written: "There is no one righteous, not even one; there is no one who understands, no one who seeks God. All have turned away, they have together become worthless; there is no one who does good, not even one." (Romans 3:10-12)

Paul's purpose was to show how everyone in the human family is a sinner alienated from God. Everett F. Harrison observes that Paul's language here "is devastatingly clear and sharp," indicating that "no exception is allowed."[6]

Paul asserted, "All have sinned and fall short of the glory of God" (3:23). By human standards, people may seem to be quite righteous. But, when judged by the standards of God's glory, all men fall hopelessly short. Even a comparatively righteous person such as Isaiah, when he had a vision of the glory of God, cried out in despair, "Woe to me! . . . I am ruined! For I am a man of unclean lips, and I live among a people of unclean lips, and my eyes have seen the King, the Lord Almighty" (Isaiah 6:5).

The fact that every person in his natural state is a sinner guilty before a holy God, and is therefore lost, has been largely forgotten today. In much of today's Christian preaching, teaching, and writing there is an emphasis on the blessings the gospel brings. The blessings are certainly very important. But there should also be a corresponding emphasis on the darkness of the separation from God in which men live apart from the gospel. This failure to emphasize both sides is one reason why many find it difficult to accept the fact that without faith in Christ there is no hope of salvation for anyone. They see the "born again" experience as a blessed "extra" to life. They don't see it as a transformation from death to life (Romans 6:23); from darkness to light (1 Peter 2:9); from rejection by God to acceptance by God (Romans 5:9-11).

GOD'S SOLUTION (ROMANS 3:21-31)
Paul expounded God's solution to the problem of the universal sinfulness of man (3:21-31). He first said that "a righteousness from God, apart from law, has been made known" (3:21). What he meant by this was that God's method of bringing people to right relation with himself is not by their earning it through fulfilling the law. Instead, "this righteousness from God comes through faith in Jesus

Christ to all who believe" (3:22). They must believe in Jesus. That is the only way to salvation.

And why is faith in Christ the only way? Paul answered this question in the next few verses. He first mentioned that all men are hopelessly lost: "For all have sinned and fall short of the glory of God" (3:23). They cannot save themselves by their own efforts. Then Paul explained that, because man cannot save himself, God in Christ acted to give him salvation.

And [we] are justified freely by his grace through the redemption that came by Christ Jesus. God presented him as a sacrifice of atonement, through faith in his blood. (3:24-25)

In these two sentences are contained some key words that explain God's plan of salvation. The first key word is *justified,* a legal term referring to a judge's act of acquitting a person on trial. When one is justified, he is treated just as if he had not sinned.

But Paul had just stated that all men are sinners. The next statement "freely by his grace" shows how God can justify sinners who fall short of his glory. The words *freely* and *grace* both indicate that justification is something we cannot earn. It is a gift. *Grace* describes the basis of this gift, something made available because of what Christ did for us. As the well-known acrostic puts it, grace is God's Riches At Christ's Expense. No one merits salvation. However good we may seem in the eyes of men, we have fallen short of the glory of God and are under condemnation. We can do nothing to save ourselves. Only God can help us. And, thank God, he does!

Here we see the flaw in the arguments of those who claim that a person's sincerity and religiousness can be a means of salvation. People are so lost in sin they are incapable of enough sincerity to merit salvation. The effects of sin upon them and upon their relationship with God are so devastating that they cannot help themselves. Their only hope is the free gift of God's grace through Christ.

By using the word *redemption,* Paul explained something of what happens when we are justified. This word essentially means deliverance from some evil by the payment of a price. It was used of the ransom paid for captives or slaves. When Jesus shed his blood, he paid the price to set us free from our bondage to sin and the powers of evil.

Paul said Christ was "presented . . . as a sacrifice of atonement" (3:25). Before man could arrive at a state of "at-one-ment" with God, a sacrifice was necessary. Man's sin and God's wrath made a relationship between God and man impossible. The sacrificing of his life enabled Christ to take away our sin by bearing it upon his body and to take away God's wrath by being punished on our behalf. Even though we have fallen short of God's glory, his righteousness has been satisfied because Jesus was punished on our behalf.

This then is what God has done for man's salvation. Paul faithfully recorded it for us to understand. When we understand, we also see that it would be impossible for man to be saved by any other way. We are too sinful to do anything to merit our salvation. But our gracious God did everything that was necessary.

This passage also mentions over and over again that faith (or belief) is the way to appropriate the benefits of Christ's work.

This righteousness from God comes through faith in Jesus Christ to all who believe (3:22).

[God is] the one who justifies the man who has faith in Jesus (3:26).

For we maintain that a man is justified by faith apart from observing the law (3:28).

There is only one God, who will justify the circumcised by faith and the uncircumcised through that same faith (3:30).

Believing is not merely giving mental assent to what Christ did and then living any way we want. Saving faith has four important steps. First, we must decide to leave behind our past life. Second, we must admit that we cannot help ourselves. Third, we must accept what Christ has done on our behalf. Fourth, we must entrust ourselves to him in this way; we accept his way of life as our way of life. So when he becomes our Savior, he also becomes our Lord.

Why is faith so important for salvation? Faith is the opposite of the basic sin that separates man from God. Man's fall took place when he chose to decide for himself what is good and what is evil. He chose to build his own system of values. So man's basic sin is independence from God. Faith is the opposite of independence from God. When one exercises faith, he rejects his own ways of saving himself and controlling his life and submits to the way God provided for him in Christ Jesus.

Here then is the gospel in a nutshell: God has, in Christ, done all that is necessary for our salvation and we must accept that by faith.

MUST THEY HEAR?

Can those who do not hear the gospel exercise saving faith? There are some who say they can. They say that what is important about Christ are his qualities. To call on his name is to place one's trust on those qualities that one discerns to be worthy of allegiance. We who know Christ know that these qualities are the qualities of Christ. According to this view, if a person repents of his selfishness and follows these principles of Christ, he will be saved even though he does not know Christ.

Much can be said against this view. The many passages explaining the need for faith present the object of faith as a Person—Christ. There is more than the principles of Christ intended here. They talk about asking a Person to be a Savior and Lord.

Other passages teach that we must hear the message of Christ before entrusting ourselves to him. Jesus said, "Whoever hears my word and believes him who sent me has eternal life and will not be condemned" (John 5:24). Before believing comes hearing. The logic of this was clearly presented by Paul:

For, "Everyone who calls on the name of the Lord will be saved." How, then, can they call on the one they have not believed in? And how can they believe in the one of whom they have not heard? And how can they hear without someone preaching to them? (Romans 10:13-14)

Later Paul added, "Faith comes from hearing the message, and the message is heard through the word of Christ" (Romans 10:17).

Some who agree with the logic presented above say, however, that this is not the only way God works. They say that there may be some who can be saved by a means other than hearing the word of Christ through a preacher or witness. We believe the arguments just presented eliminate that possibility. Yet in the next chapter we will consider some of the means they suggest and show that there are no scriptural grounds for the view that saving faith could be exercised apart from the preaching of the gospel.

DEGREES OF RESPONSIBILITY

Before closing this discussion we must point out that the Bible teaches that there will be degrees of punishment according to the degrees of responsibility of different individuals. This is a new thought to many Christians. They have learned that in God's sight sin is sin and that when it comes to the matter of salvation, there is no differentiation between big sins and small sins.

It is not the individual sins that are of eternal consequence. It is the fact that man is a sinner. If a person is dead in sin, he is dead whether he is a good person in the eyes of the world or not. We heartily agree with all this. That is why we have affirmed that, apart from faith in Christ, there is no hope for salvation for anyone.

Yet, along with this body of biblical teaching, we must also consider those Scriptures that teach that at the judgment some will receive a harsher punishment than others. Two criteria determine the severity of this punishment: the light one has received and the works he has done.

Four New Testament passages declare that the degree of light an unbeliever receives influences the degree of punishment he will receive. The first is Matthew 11:20-24, which says that Tyre, Sidon, and Sodom were destroyed for their wickedness. But they did not receive the light that Korazin, Bethsaida, and Capernaum had received. Jesus said that on the judgment day it would be more bearable for the wicked cities of Tyre, Sidon, and Sodom than for the other three cities not famous for overt wickedness.

Christ's words in Luke were even more explicit. He said that the "servant who knows his master's will and does not get ready [for his coming] or does not do what his master wants will be beaten with many blows" (Luke 12:47). He had much light, but disregarded it. "The one who does not know and does things deserving punishment will be beaten with few blows." He had enough light to be held accountable for his actions, so he was punished. But the master's will had not been explicitly communicated to him, so he received few blows. Jesus went on to give the principle behind his reasoning: "From everyone who has been given much, much will be demanded; and from the one who has been entrusted with much, much more will be asked" (12:48).

Paul first affirmed God's impartiality: "For God does not show favoritism." Then he illustrated how this impartiality is manifested in the judgment: "All who sin apart from the law will also perish apart from the law, and all who sin under the law will be judged by the law" (Romans 2:11, 12).

We note that each of these passages states that those receiving less light will be punished. But those receiving more light will be punished more severely.

The writer of Hebrews described very specifically those who reject the gospel. Their fate will be worse than those who rejected the law of Moses:

If we deliberately keep on sinning after we have received the knowledge of the truth, no sacrifice for sins is left, but only a fearful expectation of judgment and of raging fire that will consume the enemies of God. Anyone who rejected the law of Moses died without mercy on the testimony of two or three witnesses. How much more severely do you think a man deserves to be punished who has trampled the Son of God under foot? (Hebrews 10:26-29)

From these passages we conclude that those who reject the gospel, after understanding what it is, will face severe punishment. Those who have not heard the gospel will be punished for not living up to the light they received. But their responsibility is less, so their punishment also will be correspondingly less. Another body of Scripture teaches that all men will be judged according to their works. We know, of course, that a person's works will not merit salvation. But evil deeds do merit punishment unless they have been forgiven and washed away by the blood of Christ. The principle behind this fact is set forth vividly in Galatians: "Do not be deceived: God cannot be mocked. A man reaps what he sows" (6:7). The Book of Revelation describes the process of the judgment of works: "And I saw the dead, great and small, standing before the throne, and books were opened . . . . The dead were judged according to what they had done as recorded in the books" (20:12, 13). Secret acts (Romans 2:16), careless words (Matthew 12:36), ungodly acts (Jude 14, 15), in fact, all works, with no exception, will come under the judgment of God. As written in Ecclesiastes: "God will bring every deed into judgment, including every hidden thing, whether it is good or evil" (Ecclesiastes 12:14).

We should not expect a devout Buddhist, then, who made some effort to live according to his principles, to receive the same punishment as a cruel tyrant who broke whatever principles he needed to break in order to satisfy his evil desires. The Buddhist's religiousness, with its independence of God's way, was an affront to God's glory, and thus will not merit salvation. But the tyrant's tyranny was a greater affront to God's glory.

Here we find part of our answer to the questions relating to the fairness of God in saving only those who hear and respond to the gospel. Sin is such a terrible thing that no one deserves to be saved. In his mercy God saves some.

Others will be punished. But those who tried to live up to the light they had will receive less punishment.

THE URGENCY OF EVANGELISM

Realizing that those who have not heard the gospel will perish should show how urgent our evangelistic task is. If people are lost and headed for condemnation apart from the gospel, then we must hasten to share the gospel with them. Jude reflects this urgency when he wrote, "Snatch others from the fire and save them" (Jude 23).

The lostness of man apart from Christ has been a great motivation to evangelists throughout the centuries. The great missionary, Hudson Taylor, said, "I would have never thought of going to China had I not believed that the Chinese were lost and needed Christ." William Booth, the founder of the Salvation Army, said he would wish his workers might spend "one night in hell" in order to see the urgency of their evangelistic task. I trust this book will help some of God's people to rediscover the biblical doctrine of the lostness of men apart from Christ and so motivate them to be faithful in the work of evangelism.

NOTES

1. C. K. Barrett, *A Commentary on the Epistle to the Romans* (New York: Harper & Row, 1957), p. 35.

2. C. E. B. Cranfield, *A Critical and Exegetical Commentary on the Epistle to the Romans*, vol. I (Edinburgh: T. & T. Clark, Ltd., 1975), p. 116.

3. Barrett, *Romans*, p. 36.

4. F. F. Bruce, *The Epistle of Paul to the Romans, Tyndale New Testament Commentaries* (Grand Rapids: Eerdmans, 1963), p. 90.

5. Max Warren, *I Believe in the Great Commission* (London: Hodder & Stoughton, 1976), p. 157.

6. Everett F. Harrison, "Romans," *The Expositor's Bible Commentary* (Grand Rapids: Zondervan, 1976), p. 38.

CHAPTER TEN
NO OTHER WAY

There are some who accept much of what was said in the last chapter about the need to believe in Jesus Christ for salvation, but who say that there are exceptions to this principle. We should consider these supposed exceptions.

THE SINCERE SEEKER
The first supposed exception is the case of the "sincere seeker." Are there sincere seekers after God whose quest God accepts and who are saved without their hearing the gospel?

Those holding to this view cite Cornelius as such an example. They point to Peter's statement that God "accepts men from every nation who fear him and do what is right" (Acts 10:35). They say that if a person fears God and does what is right, as Cornelius did, he will be accepted by God and granted salvation. But the record of Cornelius' conversion shows that he was not saved until Peter preached to him. The angel who visited Cornelius told him that Peter "will bring you a message through which you and all your household will be saved" (Acts 11:14). The message had to be heard for salvation to be granted. Therefore, Acts 10:35 could not be implying that people such as Cornelius could be saved without hearing the gospel message. Peter expressed his surprise that Gentiles could be saved at all. We conclude with Everett F. Harrison that when Peter said that God accepts men from every nation who fear him and do what is right, he meant that even Gentiles are "suitable candidates for salvation."[1]

What we can learn from the story of Cornelius is that to a truly sincere person God will reveal the gospel even if he has to work a miracle to do so. The only means we know of through which such a revelation can come is the proclamation of the gospel of Christ. J. Oswald Sanders gives two examples worth noting of such people.[2]

The first story was originally related by Dr. N. L. Niswander in *The Alliance Weekly* of July 2, 1958. A missionary, while he was preaching, was impressed with a listener whose face expressed openness and interest.

The subject of Christ as Savior brought him delight and joy. Later, when he talked with the missionary, the man spoke of three crises in his life. The first one was of his becoming aware of the perfection and wonder of the universe. Nature revealed to him the awesome wonder of the Mighty One. The next crisis was a serious condemnation and conviction of sin. His knowledge of the grandeur of nature brought to light his own imperfections. He realized then the close relationship between the physical laws and the moral law and the holiness of God. In the third crisis he became an earnest seeker for God's answer to this confusion in his heart and mind. He testified that when he sought God's forgiveness, he was conscious of a Saviour's presence. And now, he continued, "Since I have heard you speak, I recognize in Jesus the Person who has made atonement for my sin."

Here was a modern Cornelius indeed. We note that this person responded as best he could to the light he received until he was finally led to Christ.

The next story Sanders gives was related by a missionary nurse in Thailand:

A couple came to our home in Thailand about three o'clock in
the afternoon. . . . The woman began to speak. "There is a matter which is troubling me, and I think you are the one who can
help me. . . . I had a dream about a man called Jesus. Could you
tell me who he is? . . ." The caller related her dreams and then
asked what it could mean. She knew nothing of Jesus except
that once she had heard this name. For five years she and her
husband had been seeking peace, and together they had tried to
live a holy life after the precepts of Buddha, but peace had not
come. Their neighbors called them mad for seeking so earnestly.
In a moment I asked the Lord for guidance and then for the next
three hours we turned from passage to passage of Scripture,
and the Holy Spirit guided and gave understanding. It was a thrill
beyond telling to see this simple couple perceive the deep things
of the Word of God. . . . The following Monday afternoon they
came again. Their opening words in chorus were, "We have
found peace and joy now as we never had before."

In both these stories the sincere seekers heard the gospel of Christ. Oswald Sanders quotes Dr. H. W. Frost, who
described people "who have seen 'men in white' who have
told them to go to certain cities or chapels and to believe
the doctrine which they might hear there." Then Dr. Frost
points out that "it took the going, the finding of the preacher, the hearing and believing to make them understand the
full meaning of the vision."

Dr. Frost concludes, "It is conceivable that God might
have ordained to preach the gospel directly to men
through dreams, visions and revelations. But as a matter of
fact he has not done this, but rather has committed the
preaching to men, telling them to go and disciple all
nations."[3]

We must add, however, that the overwhelming majority
of people do not seek God in this way. In fact, when the
gospel is preached to them, many reject it. Most of those

who have accepted the gospel would testify that they did not earnestly go seeking after the gospel. My experience and that of many others working among non-Christians is that seekers of the type of Cornelius are hardly ever found anywhere.

SALVATION IN OLD TESTAMENT TIMES
There is a growing number of scholars who are drawing a principle about salvation from the fact that there were Jews who were saved without the gospel before Christ came to this world. They say that in the same way people may be saved today too before the gospel is presented to them if they fear the Lord as the Old Testament saints did.

We see, however, that in Old Testament times two key features were necessary for salvation. Both these features are keys to salvation in the gospel of Christ too. So we can say that in every fundamental area, salvation in the Old Testament foreshadowed salvation in the gospel of Christ.

The first feature of Old Testament salvation is that those saved received a special revelation of God and his ways. This revelation is now recorded in the Old Testament. This revelation was often misunderstood by the Jews. But, properly understood, it is essentially similar to the revelation in the gospel of Christ. It presents a covenant relationship between God and his people, which is mercifully initiated by God and received by man through faith.

Second, in the Old Testament times, there needed to be what Carl F. H. Henry calls "a divinely approved sacrifice . . . which focuses on the Mediator—Messiah . . . if only in an elementary and preparatory sense." Henry reminds us that "the God of the Old Testament is angry with mankind in sin; only the satisfaction of his righteousness and the expiation of sin by the perfect sacrifice of the Promised Mediator renders him propitiatory." The Old Testament sacrifices foreshadowed and looked forward to this sacrifice of Christ. They propitiated God. That is, they took away his wrath against sin. Henry concludes, "A religion that speaks of forgiveness without a doctrine of substitutionary mediation and atonement has nothing in common either with Old Testament or New Testament religion."[4]

Salvation in the Old Testament, then, involved a covenant relationship with God, which required accepting God's special revelation of himself and his ways and also required the offering of sacrifices of atonement to God. These two requirements could not be fulfilled by the so-called "B.C. non-Christians" of today who have not yet heard the gospel.

Are there exceptions recorded in the Old Testament to the method of salvation outlined above? Were people saved without the help of the covenant community, its revelation, and its sacrifices? Five people have been mentioned as being exceptions.

The first of these supposed exceptions is Abraham. But he had to be an exceptional case because he was the founder of the covenant community. Yet he, too, fulfilled the two requirements mentioned above. He accepted the special revelation and he offered the atoning sacrifices. Of course, he did not receive the revelation from a human source. God spoke directly to him. But because he was such an exceptional case we would do well to be cautious about concluding from his example that God speaks directly to others, too, in bringing them to salvation.

The second so-called exception is Job. But we know so little of Job that it would be best not to arrive at conclusions about his religious background and how God revealed himself to Job. Of course, we do know that Job offered sacrifices to God (Job 1:5).

We know more about the background of the third so-called exception, Balaam. He was a non-Jewish "prophet" from Mesopotamia. We know that God did speak through him. But, as Gordon Wenham points out, the Bible does not portray him as "a good man or true believer." Wenham reminds us that "throughout the Bible, prophecy and other ecstatic spiritual gifts are regarded as signs of inspiration, but not necessarily of holiness or of a right standing with God."[5] He was among those killed when God asked the Israelites to take vengeance on the Midianites (Numbers 31:1-8). In the New Testament his name is a symbol of greed (2 Peter 2:15; Jude 11) and of participation in pagan worship and immorality (Revelation 2:14). Most certainly, Balaam is not portrayed in the Scriptures as a saved person.

The fourth example mentioned is Jethro, Moses' father-in-law, who is remembered for his advice on delegating the administration of justice (Exodus 18). We know that this man offered sacrifices to God (Exodus 18:12). While he was not a Jew, he did have close contact with the Jews and their revelation through his son-in-law, Moses. So, he is not a good example to use as evidence for the view that the unevangelized could be saved. The unevangelized whom we are considering have no contact with the gospel. Jethro had much contact with the Old Testament gospel.

The fifth example is Melchizedek, the priest-king of Salem, who blessed Abraham and received a tithe of the spoils from Abraham's victorious battle against neighboring kings. He seemed to have been in touch with God even though he was not a part of the covenant community. If he was saved, was he saved without contact with the Old Testament gospel? The text in Genesis 14 must imply that he was a friend of Abraham. An influential man like Abraham would most certainly know the king of neighboring Salem (probably Jerusalem). Could he have heard about God from Abraham? This is possible, but we cannot be sure.

Melchizedek appears so suddenly and then moves off the scene so soon that the writer of Hebrews uses this sudden appearance and disappearance as a symbol of eternity (Hebrews 7:1-3). He uses this fact as a symbol of having no beginning or end. My point is that we know too little about Melchizedek to develop a theology about the salvation of those not hearing the gospel.

We conclude that the Bible does not make any clear statement about exceptional persons to whom God speaks directly and gives salvation without their hearing the gospel. This principle can only be derived from hints and questionable examples in Scripture. The Bible does not give us sufficient grounds to entertain a hope of salvation for anyone apart from the gospel. We know that most people in the world do not seek after God as Cornelius did. We have no convincing evidence to expect that the few Cornelius-type seekers in the world could be saved apart from hearing the gospel. So, we believe that God would have us regard all people everywhere as lost and desperately in need of the gospel.

AN OPPORTUNITY AFTER THAT?

An idea often discussed is the possibility of people hearing the gospel after they die. It is said that especially those who have not heard will be given this opportunity.

Yet the whole tenor of Scripture is in another direction. We read in Hebrews: "Man is destined to die once, and after that to face judgment" (9:27). In his parable about Lazarus and the rich man, Jesus spoke about a great chasm between heaven and hell. Abraham tells the rich man, "Between us and you a great chasm has been fixed, so that those who want to go from here to you cannot, nor can anyone cross over from there to us" (Luke 16:26). Leon Morris points out that the Greek here indicates that this blocking of the way is "the purpose and not simply the result of the great chasm." This is why we have the words *so that* in the text. Morris says this statement means that "in the afterlife there is no passing from one state to the other."[6]

Over and over again in Hebrews we are told "Today is the day of salvation" (3:7, 13, 15; 4:7). Isaiah wrote: "Seek the Lord while he may be found; call on him while he is near" (55:6), implying that the day of opportunity will end for man.

Yet two texts in 1 Peter have been used to present the idea of a chance of hearing the gospel after death. Much has been written about these texts, including a whole book by a Roman Catholic scholar, William J. Dalton, whose conclusions tally closely with ours.[7] Here we will present a comparatively brief exposition of these texts.

Preaching to the Spirits in Prison (1 Peter 3:19, 20). Peter wrote that Christ "went and preached to the spirits in prison who disobeyed long ago when God waited patiently in the days of Noah while the ark was being built" (3:19, 20). Those holding to the view of the chance for salvation after death interpret these verses as saying that Christ preached the gospel to dead human beings in the abode of the dead. They say we can extend the principle emerging from this passage to build a doctrine of a chance to repent after death.

The key to understanding this text centers around the identity of the "spirits in prison" to whom Christ preached. The noun translated "spirits" *(pneuma)* is used alone here, without any qualifying words before or after it. J. N. D. Kelly

shows that in the New Testament and other Jewish literature of the time it was normally used in this way to describe
good and bad supernatural beings (e.g., Matthew 12:45;
Luke 10:20; Hebrews 1:14).[8] It is not used in this unquali-
fied way for the spirits of human beings. For this and other
reasons many scholars today identify "the spirits in prison"
with the disobedient angels of Genesis 6:1-4 who married
the daughters of men and caused much harm to the human race.[9]

Genesis 6:1-4 belongs to the same segment of Scripture
as Noah's story (6:5–9:29). That would explain the asso-
ciation of spirits with the day of Noah. The angels of Genesis 6:1-4 were a favorite topic in a lot of extra-biblical
literature of the time. Because we are unfamiliar with this
body of literature, this is alien territory for most of us. But it
was familiar territory for Peter and his readers. In fact,
these angels are mentioned in 2 Peter 2:4 and Jude 6, too.

When the angels are mentioned in 2 Peter 2:4 and Jude
6, it is in connection with their judgment. Our passage, too,
has this idea. The proclamation Christ made to the spirits
in prison is not what we would call a gospel proclamation.
The word Peter uses does not demand that we understand
it in this way. Peter did not use the world *euangelizo,* which
means "to proclaim good news." Instead he used *kerusso,*
which means "to announce." This word is often used to refer to the proclamation of the gospel. But it can also be
used without reference to the gospel (e.g., Luke 13:3; Romans 2:21; Revelation 5:2). We believe this is another
such instance of the use of this word for a proclamation of
something other than the gospel.

What is this proclamation that Christ made to the angels? In the words of Edwin Blum, it is "the announcement
of his victory and of their doom that has come through his
death on the cross and his resurrection."[10] It could have

taken place either during the days between his death and resurrection or after his ascension.

An examination of 1 Peter 3 shows that the purpose of this passage is to give encouragement to persecuted Christians. It is to remind them that Christ is victor over all evil forces by virtue of his death and resurrection. These forces may be very powerful. They may cause much havoc, as the angels did in the days of Noah. But Christ has proclaimed his victory over even those powerful foes of righteousness. So, Peter's readers do not need to fear. They can be sure that Christ will defeat the evil forces that were causing them so much hardship at that time. In the preceding paragraph, Peter had instructed his readers on how to face ill treatment. The paragraph we are studying describes the confidence the Christian has in the midst of this struggle because Jesus is victor. So, we see how identifying the spirits in prison with the angels of Genesis 6 is most natural to the context of these verses.

The Gospel Preached to the Dead (1 Peter 4:6). Peter wrote, "For this is the reason the gospel was preached even to those who are now dead, so that they might be judged according to men in regard to the body, but live according to God in regard to the spirit" (1 Peter 4:6). This verse has often been associated with the verse about the spirits in prison (1 Peter 3:19). But the vocabulary and contexts of these two verses differ very much.[11] Those holding to the view of the possibility of an offer of salvation after death say that this verse teaches that the gospel was preached to non-Christians after they died. Instead we affirm, with a host of eminent scholars, that the dead spoken of here are Christians who are now dead and that the preaching mentioned was done while they were still alive.[12]

This interpretation becomes clearer as we look at the context of this verse. First, the chapter starts with a challenge to believers to be prepared to suffer unjustly with the attitude of Christ who also suffered for the sake of righteousness (4:1). So, despite the suffering it accompanies, we must live holy lives (4:1), even though most people around us live unholy lives (4:3). In fact, unholy people do not understand our refusal to pursue unholy pleasure. They think we are strange and heap abuses on us (4:4). "But they will have to give account to him who is ready to judge the living and the dead" (4:5). Next comes the verse we are studying, which talks of a different judgment done on earth "in regard to the body," or more literally, the flesh. This is the judgment the world gives Christians, and it may even take the form of martyrdom. What Peter was saying was that, even though Christians are judged as failures in the earthly realm ("in regard to the body"), they are very much alive in the heavenly realm ("in regard to the spirit").

Now, let us look at the different phrases in this verse (4:6). First, Peter said, "The gospel was preached even to those who are now dead." It does not say that the gospel was preached to them after they died. We decide on whether it was after or before based on the context. The context makes sense if we take it as being before death. So these people, to whom the gospel was preached and who gave their lives to Christ, died in shame because of their faith. In Peter's words, they were "judged according to men in regard to the body." Yet this judgment is reversed in the heavenly realm, for they "live according to God in regard to the Spirit."

Verse 6, like the other verses in this paragraph (4:1-6), is an encouragement to believers to persevere along the path of commitment to Christ amidst suffering. In the earthly realm they may appear to be failures, but in the heavenly realm their life is complete and victorious, for earthly judgment will be reversed in that realm.

So we conclude that both 1 Peter 3:19, 20 and 4:6 do not deal with the issue of an opportunity for salvation after death.

UNANSWERED QUESTIONS ABOUT GOD'S FAIRNESS

Having read what has been written in this chapter and the preceding one, there may still remain in the mind of the reader some unanswered questions about God's fairness and justice. When confronted with this problem, we must be careful not to try to fit God into our thinking by rejecting some things the Bible teaches. Dick Dowsett has said, "Human hunches do not give us right answers about God. Neither can we learn how God would behave by looking at the way nice people do things."[13] After all, the Scriptures themselves say that God's ways and thoughts are higher than our ways and thoughts (Isaiah 55:8, 9; see also Romans 11:33, 34). So we must approach these issues humbly, realizing that God has revealed his ways to us in the Scriptures and seeking to align our thinking with God's thinking as revealed in these Scriptures.

One aspect of scriptural truth that the contemporary human mind finds difficult to grasp is the area of God's wrath. Our thinking about God's holiness falls so short of the complete truth that we have lost God's sense of the seriousness of sin. We don't fully realize how much sin is an affront to God's glory. We don't realize what an awesome and serious act of rebellion against God our independence of him is. No one deserves to be saved. It is absolute mercy that causes at least some to be saved at all.

But why do some receive this mercy while others don't? Indeed, at the moment this is a problem. Some have solved it by appealing to the doctrine of predestination.

There is strong evidence in Scripture that those who are saved were predestined for salvation by God (see especially Ephesians 1). But there is a difference of opinion about what this predestination means. Were the unsaved predestined to damnation? Did they have no chance at all? We do not believe such a conclusion is necessarily implied by the passages teaching predestination.

While some questions may still remain in our minds, we must affirm that the Bible clearly teaches the fairness of God's judgment (Genesis 18:25; Deuteronomy 10:17; 1 Peter 1:17). One day in heaven we will understand the justice of God's ways and even praise him for his judgments as those in the courts of heaven do (see Revelation 16:5-7; 19:1-3; 6:10; 11:17, 18; 18:20). Paul reminded us that "now we see but a poor reflection" (1 Corinthians 13:12). In heaven our vision is unhindered by our weaknesses and wrong perceptions. Then we will understand the reasons for God's wrath and agree with them. Oswald Sanders says, "When from eternity's vantage point we learn what he has done, we will be amazed, not at his severity, but at his mercy."[14] Paul said that at the judgment seat every mouth will be silenced and the whole world will be held accountable to God (Romans 3:19). Everyone will realize he is just in his judgment.

Before we receive this full light about God's ways, we would be wise to accept, humbly and completely, what God has revealed in his Word. We should try to solve the problems arising from what is difficult to explain (see 1 Peter 3:15), which will be a lifelong task. Karl Barth is said to have stated that all theology is *theodicy,* the vindication of the ways of God.

Because questions on some topics may still remain in our minds, we must not disregard what the Scriptures teach about them, as many have done today. People have discarded the passages that do not fit into their systems of thought, and from other passages they have drawn conclusions that fit into their systems of thought. But these conclusions read too much into the texts from which they are drawn. Their conclusions are not necessary implications of these texts. It is far more appropriate for us to accept all of Scripture and grapple with the problems we encounter from doing that rather than take the easier route of discarding some things the Scriptures teach because they do not fit in with our understanding of God.

NOTES

1. Everett F. Harrison, *Acts: The Expanding Church* (Chicago: Moody Press, 1975), p. 172.

2. J. Oswald Sanders, *How Lost Are the Heathen?* (Chicago: Moody Press, 1972), pp. 67-70.

3. Ibid., p. 70, 71.

4. Carl F. H. Henry, *God, Revelation and Authority: God Who Stands and Stays,* vol. 6 (Waco: Word Books, 1983), p. 369.

5. Gordon J. Wenham, *Numbers, The Tyndale Old Testament Commentaries* (Leicester and Downers Grove, Ill.: InterVarsity Press, 1981), p. 168.

6. Leon Morris, *The Gospel According to St. Luke, The Tyndale New Testament Commentaries* (Grand Rapids: Eerdmans, 1974), p. 254.

7. William J. Dalton, *Christ's Proclamation to the Spirits* (Rome: Pontifical Biblical Institute, 1965).

8. J. N. D. Kelly, *A Commentary on the Epistles of Peter and Jude* (n.d.; reprint, Grand Rapids: Baker Book House, 1981), p. 154. I am indebted to Kelly for many points given in this discussion.

9. E.g., Edwin A. Blum, William J. Dalton, J. N. D. Kelly, Bo Reicke, and Edward G. Selwyn.

10. Edwin A. Blum, "1 Peter," *The Expositor's Bible Commentary* vol. 12, ed. Frank E. Gaebelein (Grand Rapids: Zondervan, 1981), p. 242.

11. Ibid., p. 245.

12. E.g. Blum, Dalton, Kelly, James Moffatt, and Selwyn.

13. Dick Dowsett, *God, That's Not Fair!* (Sevenoaks: OMF Books, n.d., and Bromley: STL Books, 1982), p. 4.

14. Sanders, *How Lost,* p. 32.

CHAPTER ELEVEN
PERSUASION AND INTOLERANCE

In our study of Paul's ministry in Athens we saw that he used the method of persuasion when preaching the gospel. Evangelism in the New Testament is often specifically described as persuasion (Acts 17:2-4; 18:4, 13; 24:25; 26:28; 28:23, 24). The word *peitho*, used in most of these instances, has been defined: "to apply persuasion; to prevail upon; to win over; to persuade, bringing about a change of mind by the influence of reason or moral consideration."[1]

Persuasion is an important practice in everyday life. Donald McGavran reminds us that it is "the basis of all learning, progress and commerce."[2] Two days after her tragic death, Sri Lanka's leading English newspaper carried this statement of Indira Gandhi as its "thought for the day": "We are a democracy. We have to persuade people rather than compel them. We have to bring about a change in the outlook of people through education and persuasion."

Mahatma Gandhi once said to Stanley Jones, "Don't attempt to propagate your faith; just live it. Be like the rose, which, without a word, silently exudes its perfume and attracts the attention of the people." Dr. Jones responded by reminding Mr. Gandhi that he was the greatest propagandist of all, seeking to propagate his views on independence and freedom to the British Empire and to the whole world.[3]

DOES PERSUASION UNDERMINE FAITH?

There are many reasons why people object to the use of persuasion in evangelism. Some Christians object to it, claiming that when we reason in this way we make Christianity into an intellectual religion and so downplay the importance of faith. Our response to this charge is that the aim of persuasion is to open the door for people to exercise faith. Faith is entrusting oneself to God based on the facts of the gospel. We must accept these facts as true if we are to do so. God himself says, "Come now, let us reason together. Though your sins are like scarlet, they shall be as white as snow; though they are red as crimson, they shall be like wool" (Isaiah 1:18). Sinners needed to accept God's way as good and true before they turned to God to receive his forgiveness. So God needed to reason with them.

DOES PERSUASION UNDERMINE
THE WORK OF THE SPIRIT?

Other Christians reject persuasion because they feel it runs counter to dependence upon the Spirit in the work of evangelism. They say people are converted through the Spirit's enlightening, not through our wisdom. In support of this they cite Paul's description of his ministry in Corinth: "My message and my preaching were not with wise and persuasive words, but with a demonstration of the Spirit's power" (1 Corinthians 2:4).

Paul's point in 1 Corinthians 2:4 was that unless the Holy Spirit works through the preacher and in the listener's heart, the wisdom and eloquence of the preacher are ineffective. We heartily agree. True preaching is *Preaching in the Spirit,* the title of an excellent book on preaching by Dennis Kinlaw.[4] The evangelist must ensure that he is filled with the Spirit. *Unction* is one of the most important words in an evangelist's vocabulary. Dr. W. E. Sangster compares unction to a boat having its sails hoisted so that it moves in the same direction as the fresh wind of God's Spirit.[5] One who has unction is controlled, empowered, and directed by the Spirit. This is what makes prayer so important in the evangelist's life and ministry. Prayer deepens our ties with the Spirit and opens the door for us to do what he wishes and for him to bless what we do.

While 1 Corinthians 2:4 proclaims the primacy of the Spirit's work, it does not eliminate the need for persuasion. Paul's intention here was to contrast reliance upon the Spirit with reliance upon human wisdom. The Spirit may use wisdom and persuasion as a means of drawing a person to Christ. The Christian communicator may be the instrument used in this. So even though he works hard at persuasion, it is ultimately not his work, but the Spirit's.

Paul was, in this verse, using a rhetorical device commonly used in Scripture to indicate what is primary. Jesus said, "I did not come to judge the world, but to save it" (John 12:47). What he meant here was that the primary purpose of his coming was salvation. But in the very next verse Jesus shows that judgment was also a necessary consequence of his coming: "There is a judge for the one who rejects me and does not accept my words; that very word which I spoke will condemn him at the last day" (John 12:48). So, even though he said that he did not come to judge, he did judge. But that was not the primary reason for his coming. Similarly, in Paul's preaching, the Spirit's work is primary, not human wisdom and persuasion. But the Spirit uses these two means in the work of evangelism.

Luke's description of Paul's ministry in Corinth indicated that he did use persuasion there. "Every Sabbath he reasoned in the synagogue, trying to persuade Jews and Greeks" (Acts 18:4; see also 18:13). In fact, Paul's statement "with a demonstration of the Spirit's power" (1 Corinthians 2:4) is a fine example of the way persuasion and the Spirit's work combine in evangelism. Paul's audience in Corinth saw very clearly what God's Spirit was doing among them. This was a "demonstration" to the people. The Greek word translated "demonstration" is used of producing proofs in an argument in court. So, the working of the Holy Spirit was a means of persuasion.

This verse also reminds us that persuasion does not take place only through logical, rational argumentation but also through actions that give evidence of the reality of the gospel. This is why "signs and wonders" played such an important part in persuading non-Christians to consider Christ in whom they had no previous interest. The non-Christians saw the power of God and were persuaded of his reality. At other times hearers may sense the reality of God through a story. This is particularly appropriate when working with those from a non-Western background.

Logical argumentation is not the way the Eastern mind generally perceives truth. A brilliant defense of the gospel, using carefully reasoned logic, may leave a Sri Lankan Buddhist villager totally unimpressed. The story of Jesus healing blind Bartimaeus may enthrall him and make him seek further truth about the compassionate Christ. And this is not because he is less civilized or advanced, but because he is more civilized and advanced in a different category. One style is different, but not better, than the other.

Of course, whatever style of persuasion one uses, the presentation of the gospel is not complete until the facts of the gospel have been communicated. These we must be faithful in presenting to those to whom we witness.

DOES PERSUASION REFLECT INTOLERANCE?
Others reject persuasion because they see it as a reflection of an attitude of intolerance. This rejection is perhaps understandable, given the mood of our day. Other religions are experiencing renewal and a new evangelistic zeal. Into this environment we go, believing that the Christian faith is unique and attempting to persuade all to accept this faith. We should not be surprised if those of other faiths take offense at our claims. Another group, those who would regard our absolute claims about Christ and the persuasion resulting from it as intolerance, are those brought up in the atmosphere of relativism, an attitude that rules much of modern society. Bishop Stephen Neill has said that in this environment "tolerance is regarded almost as the highest of virtues."[6]

Yet the uniqueness of Christianity, out of which the ministry of persuasion springs, is something we cannot jettison, for it is something intrinsic to Christianity. The British historian, Arnold Toynbee, accepted the fact that the belief in uniqueness was intrinsic to Christianity. But he added that, however hard it may be, we must purge Christianity of this exclusive mind-set. Bishop Neill calls this "a very odd piece of argumentation." He said, "If Christianity is purged of something that is unique to itself, it will be transformed to something wholly other than itself."[7] He says this is like trying to remove chlorine from hydrochloric acid. If Christianity is to remain as Christianity, it must maintain a belief in its uniqueness.

Jesus Christ claimed to be the truth (John 14:6). Therefore, any system that contradicts what he has revealed is untrue and must be regarded as such. Bishop Neill calls this the "awful and necessary intolerance of truth."[8]

If a person builds his life on an untruth, we have the responsibility to direct him to the truth. And that means bringing him to the point of discarding the untruth in order to accept the truth. If we see a person trying to drink a dangerous cyanide compound, believing it to be harmless, we cannot ignore the situation by stating that this is his personal opinion which he is entitled to hold and with which we must not interfere. We would do everything in our power to persuade him against drinking the substance. John Stott asks, "How can Christians be intellectually tolerant of opinions we know to be false or actions we know to be evil?" He calls this "unprincipled indulgence."[9] Similarly, our belief in the ineffectiveness of other faiths and the effectiveness of the Christian faith in bringing salvation compels us to persuade people about the truth of the gospel of Christ.

IMPOSITION AND MANIPULATION

While the Bible upholds the value of persuasion, it also urges us to treat people with respect. Peter described the harmony between persuasion and respect well: "Always be prepared to give an answer to everyone who asks you to give the reason for the hope that you have" (1 Peter 3:15). This describes persuasion. Then Peter went on to say, "But do this with gentleness and respect" (v. 16). So the Christian is intolerant of untruth, but respectful of people.

We act in a disrespectful manner when we use imposition and manipulation in evangelism. John Stott has defined *imposition* as "the crusading attempt to coerce people by legislation to accept the Christian way."[10] We can proclaim the gospel with authority, but we must not use force to convert people. Donald McGavran says, "Intolerant persons are those who not only believe they are absolutely right, but forbid others to hold beliefs which differ from theirs. Intolerant people *force* others to believe as they do."[11]

Often, in the history of the church, Christians have been guilty of using the threat of persecution and the deprivation of rights to coerce people to accept the gospel. Stott cites the inquisition in Europe as an example of imposition. This was a special tribunal set up by the Roman Catholic church in the thirteenth century to combat heresy and was in operation for almost six centuries. After their trial, "Impenitent heretics were punished by excommunication, imprisonment or confiscation of goods, or were handed over to the State to be burned alive."[12] The history of colonialism is also dotted with regrettable examples of such imposition of Christianity in non-Christian lands with the support of colonial rulers. The biblical attitude is to respect each individual's freedom to choose the lord he would serve. God has ensured this by giving man the freedom to accept or reject the gospel. He does not force his will on anyone.

The second disrespectful means related to persuasion is *manipulation.* This, sad to say, is still quite commonly done in evangelism. We will discuss three types of manipulation here. First, manipulation takes place when the gospel is presented with the promise of aid or education as an incentive to those who will become "Christians." It is our Christian responsibility to help people in the name of Christ. But they must never be lured into making a commitment to Christianity primarily because of the prospect of aid. Our concern should be shown to people, regardless of whether they come to Christ or not, and they should know that.

Samuel Mendis was one of Sri Lanka's great evangelists, who worked among the poorest of the poor. Though he himself lived as a poor man all his life, he used funds from some Christian organizations to help raise the socio-economic conditions of the people to whom he ministered. He also faithfully preached the gospel of salvation to them. In fact, this was his primary concern. But he knew he could not, as a Christian, ignore their other needs. Yet, often while preaching, he publicly assured the people that there would be no connection between the aid received and their acceptance of the gospel. I believe many more would have made professions of commitment to Christ if there had been a closer link between commitment to Christ and the aid received. But such would have become "Christians" to serve mammon, not God!

Second, manipulation takes place when we stir people's emotions to such an extent that they respond to our invitation to follow Christ without the involvement of their mind and will. As the emotions are an important part of a person, they must be involved in the decision to follow Christ, which is a decision taken by the whole person. But there are times when only the emotions are involved in this decision. Emotions will not yield a genuine commitment to Christ. So, while we may appeal to the emotions in our preaching, we must be careful not to overdo it, especially toward the end of the proclamation when we invite people to respond to the call of Christ.

The danger of fostering "emotional" decisions for Christ also exists at evangelical youth camps, where uncommitted people are bombarded with the gospel day and night along with a packed program involving sports, drama, fellowship, and fun. The uncommitted youth does not have much time to reflect alone on the message he is receiving. He is caught up in a feverish burst of Christian activity and fellowship. He is physically and emotionally tired. The invitation is given many times a day, and he finally succumbs, but not with his whole self. When he returns to normal life, he regrets the decision he made and often reverts back to his old life. Because of this danger, we have introduced longer times of relaxation in our Youth for Christ evangelistic camps and reduced the number of times the public invitation to receive Christ is given. In this way we have tried to reduce the number of those whose decision to follow Christ is too closely tied up with the emotionally charged atmosphere of an evangelistic camp.

The third example of manipulation has been called "mind-bending." Here a person is influenced by a group leader to such an extent that he surrenders his autonomy to this other influence. Mind-bending is often practiced by the cults. It may take the form of brainwashing, where systematic indoctrination is done so that the mind is forced to think in a certain way. Mind-bending also takes place when a strong personality forces his viewpoint so powerfully that a person accepts this viewpoint only because he has no resources to resist it. Leaders with strong personalities have to beware lest they control the minds of others. This is what Adolf Hitler did with the German people. Such strong leaders would need to restrain themselves so as to ensure that the people they influence can make free choices in response to the truth.

AUTHORITY IN AN AGE OF UNCERTAINTY
Underlying our case for persuasion in evangelism is the belief that we have a clear message, which we know to be

true and which we can proclaim with authority. In evangelism what we proclaim is not a message we have created but the authoritative Word of God, which has been clearly communicated in the Scriptures.

Yet, the cause of the gospel has been greatly hindered by evangelists who have spoken authoritatively on topics about which the Bible is not clear. There have been times when the gospel message has been closely linked with a particular scheme of eschatology or with a certain political ideology or social program. With time, the schemes or programs of these speakers were shown to be incorrect. Christ did not return on a stipulated date. Some left- or right-wing government failed to solve the problems of the nation. The doctrine of Aryan supremacy proved to be an evil myth.

Every person has a right to share his opinions about a given topic. But each opinion may not have been directly derived from the Scriptures. We must share with authority all truths directly drawn from the Scriptures. These truths may be in the spiritual realm, such as man's need for a relationship with God. They may be in the social realm, such as God's hatred of racism. Or they may be in any other realm. But if there is no clear teaching in the Scriptures about something, we must not claim biblical authority for it.

Much harm has resulted through people who have misused this principle by preaching authoritatively on subject matter that is not backed by the authority of God's Word. Some, seeing this misuse of authority, have stopped believing in the possibility of knowing absolute truth. Many have been disappointed or have turned cynical after realizing the wrongness of the so-called "absolute truths" they were taught. Their turning from absolutes helps them fit in well with the atmosphere of relativism that rules our age.

This atmosphere of relativism in which we live has done

much to breed unhealthy absolutism in the church. People have become so insecure amidst the relativity and lack of conviction surrounding them that they have overreacted by almost deifying the act of believing. They feel the answer to the uncertainty around them is to speak authoritatively about everything. The process then has gone full circle—unfounded absolutism has created cynicism and attitudes of relativism, which has been responded to by more unfounded absolutism.

God in his sovereignty has not disclosed all the riches of his wisdom to us. He has given us enough to have a completely fulfilled life. But he has not given us clear-cut answers to many questions, such as the exact date of Christ's return. We do not need to be afraid to say that we don't know the answers to these questions.

I have heard people say, "He may be wrong about his convictions, but at least he is sure about what he believes." They think confidence is commendable even though it may be baseless. This attitude is dangerous ground for a Christian to tread. The biblical Christian's commitment is to truth and not primarily to the act of believing. We are committed to believing the truth and nothing else. We know that God has, in the Scriptures, revealed truth that is inspired, inerrant, and absolute. It is a complete revelation, which means in it is found everything that is necessary to complete faith and practice (2 Timothy 3:16, 17). But this is not an encyclopedic revelation, so it does not tell us everything, such as the date of Christ's return. Therefore, it has become necessary for the church to grapple with issues like the time of the tribulation, the relationship between church and state, and the mode of baptism. Yet, exact solutions to these are not essential for a complete life. John Wesley, Charles Spurgeon, and D. L. Moody had different views on the Millennium, but all three of them were careful students of the Word, great Christians, and effective evangelists.

So, we do not need to be afraid of admitting to uncertainty about certain details and about discarding ideas we have held to, which we find later to be untrue. These "uncertainties" pale into insignificance in the light of the glorious certainties of the gospel. We believe these certainties with all our hearts. We have experienced their transforming influence upon our lives. We know they are inerrant, so we dare not tamper with them. The inerrancy of these truths also makes us unafraid to proclaim them with authority and hesitant to place on par with them anything that is not clearly taught in the Scriptures.

We know how God's authority accompanies the proclamation of these certainties and enlightens the blind, quickens the spiritually dead, comforts the sorrowing, and gives release to guilty sinners. It is no wonder then that Paul should proclaim, "I am compelled to preach. Woe to me if I do not preach the gospel!" (1 Corinthians 9:16).

The Christian approaches the unbeliever with a sense of authority, an authority not intrinsic to himself, but wholly derived from God whose Word he proclaims. With such authority, he had the confidence to practice the ministry of persuasion. He has no hesitancy to call the unbeliever to leave his past life and follow Christ as his only Lord despite the great costliness of that step.

NOTES

1. W. E. Vine, *An Expository Dictionary of New Testament Words,* vol. III (Old Tappan, N.J.: Fleming H. Revell Co., 1940).

2. Arthur F. Glasser and Donald A. McGavran, *Contemporary Theologies of Mission* (Grand Rapids: Baker, 1983), p. 231.

3. Cited in J. T. Seamands, *The Supreme Task of the Church* (Grand Rapids: Eerdmans, 1964), p. 77.

4. Dennis F. Kinlaw, *Preaching in the Spirit* (Grand Rapids: Zondervan, 1985).

5. W. E. Sangster, *The Approach to Preaching* (1951; reprint, Grand Rapids: Baker, n.d.), pp. 24-37.

6. Stephen Neill, *Crises of Belief* (London: Hodder and Stoughton, 1984), p. 30.

7. Stephen Neill, *Creative Tension* (London: Edinburgh House Press, 1959), p. 11.

8. Ibid, p. 12.

9. John R. W. Stott, *Involvement: Being a Responsible Christian in a Non-Christian Society,* vol. 1 (Old Tappan, N.J.: Fleming H. Revell Co., 1984, 1985), p. 78.

10. Ibid., p. 75.

11. McGavran, *Contemporary Theologies,* p. 224.

12. Stott, *Involvement,* p. 75.

CHAPTER TWELVE
UNIQUENESS AND ARROGANCE

We have affirmed many times already that man's one hope for salvation is belief in Christ. But this affirmation is not very popular today. In this chapter and the next we will discuss two objections to our claim about the uniqueness of Christianity. First, such a claim is said to reflect an attitude of arrogance. Second, this claim is associated with the conquests of imperial powers that used force to win people to a religion in a process that came to be called proselytism.

Many today are saying that the Christian claim to uniqueness contradicts the attitude of humility Christ exemplified. They say it is arrogance that causes us to hold that our way is the only way and that others should leave their religions to join "our side." Is this so? Below we will give four reasons showing that biblical evangelism is incompatible with arrogance even though it maintains its authority and its absolute claims about the gospel.

THE EXAMPLE OF CHRIST
We start with the example of Christ. It is he whom we proclaim. He is our model for ministry. He is the one who told

us to go and preach. His ministry was characterized by power and authority (Matthew 7:29). He called people to forsake everything that hindered them and follow him (Luke 18:22). His fishermen disciples did just that when they left their nets to follow him (Mark 1:16-20).

Yet Christ's life was also distinguished by its humility. He said he "did not come to be served, but to serve, and to give his life as a ransom for many" (Matthew 20:28; Mark 10:45). At the last supper, when his disciples were disputing among themselves as to which of them was the greatest, he told them, "I am among you as one who serves" (Luke 22:27). Then he shocked them by dressing himself as a household servant and washing their feet, a servant's task (John 13:3-12).

Peter refused to accept such a service from the Messiah. He was reflecting an attitude toward Christ similar to that of many of Christ's contemporaries. They could not reconcile his humility with his authority. If he was Messiah he should come as a king. A king cannot be a servant.

Contemporary critics of evangelism are making the same mistake that Christ's contemporaries made, though from a different perspective. Jesus' critics said that because he came as a humble servant, he could not have authority. Evangelism's critics say that evangelists speak with so much authority that they cannot be humble. Christ demonstrated that authority and humility can harmoniously coexist.

Jesus affirmed, "All authority in heaven and on earth has been given to me" (Matthew 28:18), a statement of absolute authority. Then he told his disciples, "Therefore go and make disciples of all nations" (28:19). From his position of authority he commissioned his disciples to the work of evangelism. Then he said, "Surely I will be with you always" (28:20). He is with us as our strength and comfort and teacher. When we go out to do the work of evangelism we not only go under his commission, but we also follow him. Yet he is a servant Lord who said, "Learn from me, for I am gentle and humble in heart" (Matthew 11:29). So if we follow Christ we too must be humble. But we must also boldly proclaim with authority his lordship among the nations.

Paul demonstrated this combination of authority and humility beautifully. "For we do not preach ourselves [humility], but Jesus Christ as Lord [authority], and ourselves as your servants for Jesus' sake [humility]" (2 Corinthians 4:5). Paul was humble enough to tell the Corinthians, some of whom were rebelling against him, that he was their servant or slave. He makes a similar statement in Ephesians: "Although I am less than the least of all God's people, this grace was given me: to preach to the Gentiles the unsearchable riches of Christ" (3:8).

THE NATURE OF OUR MESSAGE
Just as the example of Christ makes arrogance incompatible with biblical evangelism, so does the gospel we proclaim. The gospel has as its foundation God's greatness and holiness. It tells us how far above us God is. Through the gospel we realize that because of sin we have fallen short of God's glory (Romans 3:23). Until we come to the point of despairing of our ability to save ourselves, the gospel will have no impact upon us. This is why Jesus said, "Unless you change and become like little children, you will never enter the kingdom of heaven" (Matthew 18:3). The gospel presents us with truths about God and ourselves that must make us humble. Yet along with this humility the Christian has a strong assurance of his own salvation, but not because of any goodness of his own. It is because he

has despaired of his efforts to save himself and has trusted in the sufficient work of Christ.

When someone asked Mahatma Gandhi what he thought about E. Stanley Jones, Gandhi replied, "He's a good man, but he's too proud of his religion." When Stanley Jones heard this he said that Gandhi was right, according to his own convictions. To Gandhi, salvation was the result of hard work. Earning salvation is as hard as trying to empty an ocean of water with one's hands. Jones was saying that a person who has assurance of salvation can be proud of it. But the Christian cannot be proud of himself, knowing that his salvation is a work of God's grace and not an achievement of his own. Gandhi never accepted the Christian doctrine of salvation by grace, so he would have regarded the Christian's confidence in his salvation as arrogance.

The gospel not only leads us to despair of our abilities but also produces within us an immense gratitude. When we realize all that Christ has done in us, despite our unworthiness, we are overwhelmed with gratitude to God. Gratitude and arrogance cannot exist together. Gratitude tells us we are recipients. It points to our unworthiness. Arrogance would suggest that one thinks he is worthy.

Gratitude also causes us to share the gospel of Christ boldly. We want others to experience this great thing that Christ has done in us. This truth is beautifully illustrated in a story my teacher, Dr. J. T. Seamands, loved to tell about a clubfooted boy in England. He lived in a small town with his widowed mother. Because of his deformity he could not walk properly. A businessman, who was a friend of the family, visited them one day and told them of a doctor in London who was having great success in operating on young people with club feet. "If you will give me permission," said the friend, "I will take your son to London and see what this doctor can do for him. I will take care of all the expenses." The mother gratefully accepted the offer.

The boy was taken to London. The operation was a success. The businessman kept the mother informed of her son's progress. Finally she got a telegram saying that the businessman and her son would be returning by train.

The mother could hardly believe her eyes as she saw the son walking up to her. He leaped into her arms and started to say, "Mother, I will . . ." but that is as far as he got. The mother stopped him and said, "Son, don't say a word. Just run up and down the platform and let Mother see how you can do it."

He ran up and down once or twice and then went to his mother and began to say something. But again she cut him short and had him run up and down the platform. Finally, the mother was satisfied and the son was able to say what he wanted to say. "Mother, I will never be satisfied until you meet that doctor in London. He's the most wonderful man in the world."[1]

Evangelism is just like that. It is a grateful person sharing with another what Christ has done in his life and can do in this other person's life too. As D. T. Niles used to say, "Evangelism is one beggar telling another beggar where to find bread."

We know beyond a doubt that people need to be converted more than anything else in the world. A young woman in Latin America came up to Stanley Jones at the close of a meeting and said, "You are happy with Christ; now show me how to be happy without Christ." His reply was, "I'm sorry, but I don't know how you can be happy without Christ. Can a railway train be happy without rails, the eye without light, the lungs without air, the heart without love?"

Jones said, "Man is made for conversion. As the duck is made for water, the bird is made for the air, the heart is made for love, the aesthetic nature is made for beauty. When you are converted you find Christ, you find yourself, your Homeland."[2] These are bold claims to make about the gospel. But the nature of the gospel demands such boldness. Through it is communicated man's only hope for salvation—Jesus Christ.

THE NATURE OF CHRISTIAN MINISTRY

The third reason that bold evangelism is incompatible with arrogance comes to light as we consider the nature of our ministry as evangelists. Our ministry is a gift to us from God. Like our salvation, it is something we do not deserve. Paul said, "Through God's mercy we have this ministry" (2 Corinthians 4:1). The word *mercy* points to our helplessness. Whatever success we have is because of him, not ourselves. So we can have no place for arrogance in evangelistic ministry.

But because evangelism is Christ's ministry we are bold. Paul said he had confidence about his ministry through Christ before God (2 Corinthians 3:4). But he immediately added "Not that we are competent to claim anything for ourselves, but our competence comes from God" (3:5). There was boldness, but not pride.

How is it then that so many evangelists are lacking in humility? We often find evangelists who are touchy individualists, easily getting hurt and upset about the way they are treated. They push their names forward, sometimes not entirely honestly. Their preaching serves to exalt themselves and their reputation. They thrive on the praise of men.

Some of these evangelists, lacking in humility, even seem to have a fruitful ministry. How is this? Possibly because there is a definite gift from God that is being used, even though the medium is unsuitable. But more probably, they are being used because the gospel they proclaim is so powerful in itself that even though the vessel through which it is communicated is unsuitable, the message has power. A Christian doctor once told me, "I was converted through the ministry of a fraud." The point he was making is that there is power in the gospel that sometimes overrides the power of the bad example of an evangelist.

Yet, these bad examples of pride do significantly damage the cause of Christ. They give ammunition to the critics of the gospel. They make it difficult for the sincere doubter to come to Christ. The lives of proud people proclaim a gospel that is no gospel at all.

What a relief and joy it is to say that the truly great evangelists are humble men. I think of Leighton Ford, Robert Coleman, J. T. Seamands, John Stott, Victor Manogarom, and Sri Lanka's own Samuel Mendis. The impression they left with me was not of their obvious gifts, but of their humility. Such a testimony has also been noted about this generation's most prominent mass evangelist, Billy Graham.

Certainly, Paul exemplified this spirit of humility. We know of his strong personality, of how he thundered against wrong teaching in a most unaccommodating manner. Modern advocates of tolerance are embarrassed by the way he insisted on fidelity to the gospel he preached. They wish verses such as Galatians 1:8 were not found in the Bible. There Paul said, "Even if we or an angel from heaven should preach a gospel other than the one we preached to you, let him be eternally condemned!"

But notice how he responded when some less honorable evangelists "preach Christ out of selfish ambition, not sincerely, supposing that they can stir up trouble for [Paul] while [he was] in chains" (Philippians 1:17). He did not thunder as he did when the gospel was diluted. He said, "But what does it matter? The important thing is that in every way, whether from false motives or true, Christ is preached. And because of this I rejoice" (1:18). He was rejoicing when his name was being slandered because what drove him in ministry was not the protection of his name but the glory of God. And God is glorified when the gospel is preached, a fact that overshadowed his disappointment over the slandering of his name.

THE NATURE OF CHRISTIAN REVELATION

A fourth reason why authority in evangelism and humility go hand in hand lies in the nature of the Christian revelation. The Bible claims that God has spoken supremely and completely in Christ (Hebrews 1:1-4). Christ claimed to be the truth and said that no one comes to the Father but by him (John 14:6). Stephen Neill points out that this "does not mean that [Jesus] was stating a number of good and true ideas." Neill says, "It means that in him the total structure, the inmost reality, of the universe was for the first time and forever disclosed."[3]

One of the implications of the Christian claim to absolute and complete revelation is that it judges the sacred writings of the other faiths. It eliminates them from the place of uniqueness given to the gospel of Christ. They may contain *truths*. But Christ is *the truth*. There are some who hold to a "broader" view of revelation that places non-Christian scriptures on a par with the Christian Scriptures. They say it is arrogant to claim that the Christian Scriptures are absolute and unique. With respect, I wish to state the opposite view, that the real arrogance is for created human beings to refuse to accept humbly what God the Creator has stated about the absolute and unique gospel of Christ.

The evangelist proclaims his message with authority because of his confidence in the wisdom of God who has revealed the gospel. But he does so with humility because he knows this message has not come from his wisdom but from the wisdom of God.

Here, then, are four reasons why biblical evangelism is incompatible with arrogance. The Master who is our example, the gospel that we proclaim, the ministry that we exercise, and the revelation God has given us all drive us to what Hendrik Kraemer has called "a remarkable combination of downright intrepidity [boldness] and of radical humility"[4] in our attitude to those of other faiths.

NOTES

1. J. T. Seamands, *The Supreme Task of the Church* (Grand Rapids: Eerdmans, 1964), pp. 78ff.

2. E. Stanley Jones, *A Song of Ascents* (Nashville: Abingdon Press, 1968), p. 32.

3. Stephen Neill, *Crises of Belief* (London: Hodder & Stoughton, 1984), p. 32.

4. Hendrik Kraemer, *The Christian Message in a Non-Christian World* (1938; reprint, Grand Rapids: Kregel Publications, 1969), p. 128.

CHAPTER THIRTEEN
CONVERSION AND PROSELYTISM

By now it should be clear that we view evangelism with conversion as a goal. We want to see people leave their former faiths, whether they are secular or religious faiths, and follow Christ as their only Lord. Conversion, however, is not a popular idea today among many Christians and non-Christians. One of Sri Lanka's most respected scholars, Dr. G. P. Malalasekera, a Buddhist, said, "Conversion . . . is an ugly word. To us in this country, it has all manner of undesirable associations, of force, of bribery and corruption, of denationalization, of the exploitation of poverty and ignorance and greed, of disease and helplessness."[1]

PROSELYTISM DESCRIBED
What Dr. Malalasekera was describing was not conversion but proselytism. Dr. J. T. Seamands differentiates between proselytism and conversion. "Proselytism is an outer change of label: it is purely *horizontal*—a shift in position along the same plane. Conversion is an inner change of *life*—wrought by God. It is primarily *vertical*—a change in position from one level to another."

Dr. Seamands tells the story of the conversion of a Muslim university student who, after carefully studying the New Testament, became convinced that Jesus was the Savior. Shortly after he was baptized as a Christian, some of his student friends met him and asked, "Ahmed, we hear that you have changed your religion; is that so?" Quick as a flash he answered, "Oh no, you've got it all wrong. I haven't simply changed my religion. My religion has changed me!" "That's conversion," says Dr. Seamands, "an inner change of life."[2]

Proselytism has taken place often in the history of the church. Whenever people become Christians for reasons that do not touch the core of the gospel, proselytism has taken place. It took place often when so-called Christian countries ruled other nations. Many became Christians because it was economically and socially advantageous to do so. Sometimes political pressure was exerted on non-Christians and people became Christians to save their skin and not their soul. Some people have felt that colonialism helped in evangelism. Certainly we can affirm that the Sovereign God uses all situations to work out some good. For example, he used the treachery of Joseph's brothers to save the family of Jacob. But it would be wrong to call colonialism a God-appointed means for the progress of the gospel. Christianity did not need the protection and support of imperialist powers in order to survive and thrive.

Colonialism differs greatly from the very spirit of evangelism. Evangelists are servants. Colonialists are masters. Evangelists identify with the culture of others. Colonialists impose their culture upon others. Evangelists take up a cross of suffering upon themselves. Colonialists inflict suffering on others. Evangelists give of themselves, their comforts, their wealth, and their rights. Colonialists grab prestige, wealth, and power.

Today in Sri Lanka the church is experiencing the consequences of having depended on colonial powers for its survival. After almost 350 years of Protestant presence in the land, more than 300 of those years being during the rule of "Protestant" nations, only 0.7 percent of our population belongs to the Protestant church. The gospel simply failed to take solid root in Sri Lanka. Following independence from the British, many who had proselytized to Christianity reverted back to Buddhism. Today we have a Protestant church that has been described as one of the weakest and most nominal in Asia.[3]

We may contrast the church in Korea with the church in Sri Lanka. They were never on the side of the colonial rulers, and they suffered much as a result. When we go out with the gospel into the interior of Sri Lanka, we are called traitors because we are supposed to have been stooges of the foreign powers who ruled Sri Lanka. The patriotism of the Korean Christians was never questioned like this. That church is thriving and growing numerically at a speed that is almost too difficult to conceive.

That most noble of causes, the missionary cause, has fallen into disrepute because people associate it with imperialism. In a book, *The Revolt in the Temple,* written to commemorate 2,500 years of Buddhism in Sri Lanka, the author claims, "In their imperialistic march, the Western powers had found the missionaries to be their best allies." He quotes an African who is credited with having said, "The Christian preacher comes and says, 'Look up,' and when we look down again the land is gone."[4] This criticism is certainly unfair, but it demonstrates what happens when colonialism is linked with Christianity.

I fear that some of the recent additions to the church in Asia may be categorized more under proselytism than under conversion. Some have joined the church because the

Christians were very generous with money. So they changed religions in order to gain wealth. Some have come attracted by the Western or upper-class life-style of the English-speaking Christians. They thought that associating themselves with the Christians would help them to climb the social ladder. Some saw that the Christian leaders were willing to look for employment for them and thought they might have a better chance of securing a job if they became Christians. A lady told me that she was offered a job and the prospect of a trip abroad if she joined a certain church.

I once talked to an eminent Buddhist educator from Sri Lanka who had worked in a Muslim country for a few years on a United Nations assignment. He told me how a Muslim friend of his complained about the way poor Muslims in this land had become Christians, lured by the aid the Christians had given. The Buddhist then had told his Muslim friend: "Don't get too upset about this. These people have become Christians only so that they can get their basic necessities of food, shelter, and clothing. This you Muslims could not give them. But, though they have taken on the Christian label, they are still Muslims at heart. Though they call themselves Christians, they will die as Muslims."

These examples show how some people outside the church view conversion. Indeed, there are some who have joined the church in this way. But they are proselytes, not converts.

Even some of those testifying to a "born again" experience in the West may not have truly experienced conversion. The reasons they are "Christians" have nothing to do with the core of the gospel. They came to Christ not with a view to having their sins forgiven and making Christ the Lord of their lives. They came for a spiritual "high," an experience that could help counteract the boredom and unfulfillment they were experiencing. Subjective experience is an important means God uses to get the attention of irreligious people. But if it stops with the "high" and leaves out repentance and the lordship of Christ, it is only an experience. It is not conversion. The basic problem of man, the problem of selfishness, has not been attacked. Because this so-called convert has begun to participate in the activities of the church, his selfishness may now express itself in a religious form. But it is still selfishness. The spiritual "high" has failed to touch the inner core of the person's life, so he is essentially an unconverted person.

SUFFERING AND EVANGELISM

How grateful we are in Sri Lanka to know that the church began among an oppressed people that were ruled by imperial Rome. The early church had no political, social, or economic clout. People did not become Christians for this type of gain. In fact, suffering and persecution were always associated closely with its growth. Dr. Robert Coleman has said that despite the witness of history, suffering, which has been a prominent factor in church growth, has been virtually overlooked in modern church growth literature. He calls suffering the hidden factor of growth that the modern affluent mind has had difficulty in comprehending.

On my visits to the West I am sometimes tempted to envy the church there when I see its facilities and resources. But then I am reminded of the call of the church in Asia to suffer. That privilege we must not forfeit. Paul said, "Everyone who wants to live a godly life in Christ Jesus will be persecuted" (2 Timothy 3:12). Now, this must apply to the West, too. So true Christians in Western lands will also suffer because of their commitment to Christ if they take the commitment seriously. Their suffering, however, may come in more subtle forms than in the East, making true discipleship all the more challenging.

The church in China gives us a good example of the principle of suffering. Some of the greatest waves of church growth were closely associated with the church's powerlessness rather than its power, with its suffering rather than its earthly prosperity. One such wave of growth came following the Boxer uprising of 1900. The Christian missionaries had received protection from Western powers who were exploiting the Chinese people. So the Chinese people associated Christianity with the West. And when they rebelled, they massacred the Christians. Probably as many as 30,000 Chinese Christians died. But with the Western force the uprising was quelled. The Chinese were forced by the Western powers into agreeing to pay high compensation for losses. Hudson Taylor's China Inland Mission and some other Christians refused this compensation in accordance with the spirit of Christ. Dr. Arthur Glasser explained what happened:

They neither filed claims nor accepted compensation when it was offered. The Chinese were amazed. In Shansi province a government proclamation was posted far and wide extolling Jesus Christ and his principles of forbearance and forgiveness. This official endorsement served to diminish the antiforeign spirit of the people and contributed not a little to the growth of the church in China in the years that followed.[5]

In more recent years the church in China has experienced one of the most phenomenal movements of church growth in the history of Christianity. About thirty-five years ago, Mao Tse-tung took over, expelled all missionaries, and forced the church to go underground. Christians all over the world prayed with sad hearts for their brothers and sisters in China. As news did not come out of China about the church, no one knew how it was doing under such difficult circumstances.

Then the government began to liberalize its policies. Christians were able to go in and see what was happening. What they saw amazed them. In about thirty-five years the number of Christians had grown from less than 5 million to 50 million (some put it as high as 100 million). Most of these Christians meet not in comfortable church buildings but in the fifty thousand or so house churches in the country.[6]

The point we have been trying to make is that earthly powers, be they social, political, or economic, are not necessary for evangelism to thrive. When earthly power and evangelism have combined, proselytism has taken place. History has shown us that some of the greatest thrusts of evangelism with genuine conversions took place when the church was bereft of earthly power.

I believe the above evidence has a message to give those who are tempted to leave difficult situations because the "doors are closing" for public evangelism. The doors may close for the traditional means of evangelism, but governments cannot stop the winsome witness of individuals filled with God's Spirit, those who share the gospel with their friends and are willing to die for this gospel. The early church, the churches of China, of Korea, of Uganda, and a host of other countries, testify to this fact.

EVIDENCES OF CONVERSION

How do we know that a person has been truly converted? In our work in Youth for Christ over the past years, we have worked a lot with unreached people. We have seen many of them profess commitment to Christ. Some have proved to be true believers while others were seen after a time to have made this "commitment" for reasons unworthy of the gospel.

Five signs have emerged out of these experiences that we have found give evidence of true conversion. These are not infallible pointers to true conversion, nor are they the only evidences of conversion. Yet, they have helped us in distinguishing a convert from a proselyte. We may describe them in John the Baptist's words as the "fruit in keeping with repentance" (Matthew 3:8); or in the words of Paul, as actions that "prove their repentance" (Acts 26:20). They are not necessary conditions for conversion. They are rather evidences that conversion has indeed occurred.

First, we must find out whether this person has understood that salvation is a gift of grace. Some accept the Christian religion, attracted to the life of Christ or by the lives of practicing Christians or by the prospect of economic or some other gain. They change religions, but there has been no inner work of grace wrought by the Holy Spirit. In place of the rituals and practices of their old religion, they have taken on the rituals and practices of Christianity.

Some of these people sincerely try to follow their new religion—in their own strength. Soon they encounter temptation, doubt, and suffering. They do not have the resources to weather these storms. Their Christianity was entirely a personal act of self-effort. When they don't have the personal strength to face trials, some of them conclude that Christianity does not work, and they give it up altogether. Others live defeated lives while remaining in the Christian community. Their focus had always been on their decision and effort. When that failed them, they either gave up Christianity or settled for a defeated life.

But these people had never accepted Christianity. To accept Christianity is to accept Christ. It is to hand over one's life to Christ and to ask him to save and to take control.

When this happens, there is an inner change wrought by God, and an experience of "life . . . to the full" (John 10:10), and strength to face up to challenges to the faith.

A second evidence of conversion is the willingness of the convert to make Christ his only Lord. He is willing to give up the idols in his life, secular and religious (1 Thessalonians 1:9). He is willing to stop worshiping at the temple or to stop looking for guidance from his horoscope when he is told that Christians don't do such things. If he shuns these practices of his former life, then we have evidence that he is no longer trusting in another god for salvation and that he has placed his trust in Christ alone.

Third, this person is willing to obey Christ, even when it is costly to do so. The way of obedience calls us to deny ourselves and to take up our cross. Christ said that it was the only way to follow him (Mark 8:34). As a true Christian grows in his understanding of Christ, he realizes that there are more areas in his life that are not pleasing to Christ. He may have yielded many of these areas when he committed his life to Christ. Repentance is a condition for salvation, not just an evidence of it. So, when he came to Christ, he repented of his past. However, God does not show us every single area of disobedience in our lives when we first come to him. Such a vision would devastate us. As we grow in the faith, God shows us many more areas that need to be yielded.

So, when a true believer finds that he cannot resort to unscrupulous business practices, he is willing to jeopardize his future by changing his ways. When he realizes that Christians cannot underpay their workers, he is willing to reduce his profits by giving his employees a fair wage. He is willing to look like a fool in society by loving his enemies. He is willing to forsake his inherited tradition of race or caste bigotry.

Are we advocating salvation by works by emphasizing these aspects of obedience? No. We are simply following the guidelines laid down by Christ who said, "Not everyone who says to me, 'Lord, Lord,' will enter the kingdom of heaven, but only he who does the will of my Father who is in heaven" (Matthew 7:21). James said, "Faith without deeds is dead" (James 2:26). If a person's life does not accord with the life of Christ, it means he has not exercised saving faith.

The fourth sign is an amplification of the third. The person is willing to pay the price of love. When a person enters the Christian community, often the first thing that impresses him is the warmth of Christian fellowship. He revels in the love he receives from his fellow Christians and gives himself to costly service within this group. There is a certain thrill in paying the price of costly service. People need to give themselves to a cause to feel important. Christianity becomes that cause.

After some time, however, the initial thrill of service dies off. Then there comes the call to persevere in service amidst tiredness, in barren fields with no visible fruit. We begin to observe the weaknesses of our fellow Christians and long-suffering needs to be exercised. With service also comes criticism, misunderstanding, and the humiliation of apparent failures. Then there is the call to give sacrificially of our possessions to the work of God.

Such challenges can be met only if there is *agape* love implanted by God in the person. This kind of love is able to survive after the initial thrill of service and fellowship is gone. Its source is something deeper than service or fellowship. Its source is the indwelling Christ, who has so energized us that we can say, "Christ's love compels us" (2 Corinthians 5:14). If Christ has truly come to dwell in a person, then Christ's love will work itself out in his life, helping him to love when it is difficult to love.

Fifth, this person has a desire to study the Scriptures. The Bible is the nourishment of the new Christian. If he is a newborn babe, he must want food for nourishment and growth (1 Peter 2:2). If he does not desire this food, then perhaps he has not been born. The seed of eternal life has not been implanted in him, giving him a new destiny—to be like Christ. This destiny creates in him a thirst to know how to be Christlike. He discovers that the Bible is the source of this knowledge and he feeds on the Scriptures. I have encountered many so-called converts who are very willing to pray and also ask others to pray for them. But they are not interested in reading the Bible. They came to Christ to get a blessing. Prayer to them is the way to get this blessing, so their prayer life is essentially an expression of selfishness. These people are not interested in making Christ Lord of their lives, so obedience is not a big issue. Thus, the Bible also did not have a high place in their lives. When these praying people found out that following Christ was costly, they refused to pay the price. When they came to Christ, they had not bargained for a cross. Instead, they came for a blessing.

I have left out prayer as one of the signs of conversion because I find many "proselytes" are willing to pray. But, I must hasten to add, a truly converted person would become a person of prayer. A relationship has been established with God and prayer is one of the deepest expressions of that relationship. But his prayer time will not be merely a recitation of requests for himself. It will take the form of a two-way conversation between two people who love each other deeply.

As we said before, these five *evidences* of conversion

are not *conditions* for conversion. A person does not need to exhibit all these qualities perfectly before we can pronounce him saved (actually only God can make such a pronouncement). But one who is indeed saved would be moving in a direction that would result in his life reflecting these five signs.

Before we end this discussion, we must point out that there is no one who comes to Christ out of pure motives. Many dynamic Christians who were converted through Youth for Christ in Sri Lanka are quite embarrassed when they remember what it was that first brought them to our meetings. If our motives were totally pure, we could boast that we were worthy to receive our salvation. But we know that no one is worthy of salvation. In fact, in our fallen state we are not capable of totally pure motives. But God takes us along with our mixed motives and uses the small mustard seed of faith found there to mediate his gift of eternal life. God uses this little spark of seeking after him as a foothold to get into our lives and begin his work of transformation. He helps us overcome our mixed motives and causes us to demonstrate in our lives the fruit of conversion we have described above.

A discussion of conversion is a fitting way to end a book on the Christian attitude to other faiths. Such a book should move beyond theoretical discussions. As Stanley Jones has affirmed so often, "Man is made for conversion."[7] Until he is converted, he has not discovered his reason for existing. Conversion takes place when Christ transforms our lives. So the Christian approaches any discussion on religion from the perspective of conversion. It has made him a new creation, and everything in an unconverted person cries out for this new creation. Evangelism proclaims the way to receive this new creation.

Notes

1. Quoted in D. C. Vijayavardhana, *Dharma-Vijaya or The Revolt in the Temple* (Colombo: Sinha Publications, 1953), p. 500.

2. J. T. Seamands, *Tell It Well: Communicating the Gospel Across Cultures* (Kansas City: Beacon Hill Press, 1981), p. 62.

3. P. F. Johnstone, *Operation World* (Bromley, Kent: STL Publications, 1978), p. 127.

4. Vijayavardhana, *The Revolt in the Temple,* p. 499.

5. Arthur F. Glasser, "China," *The Church in Asia,* ed. Donald E. Hoke (Chicago: Moody Press, 1975), p. 171.

6. Figures taken from Thomas Wang, "Their Finest Hour," *Chinese Around the World,* Jan. 1983, p. 2.

7. E. Stanley Jones, *A Song of Ascents* (Nashville: Abingdon Press, 1968), p. 32.

SUBJECT INDEX

INDEX OF PERSONS

SCRIPTURE INDEX